My Brooklyn Bridge

My Brooklyn Bridge

Take a Journey with Me as I Build a Career in Dentistry, Inventing, and Furniture

Jeffrey M. Hills

NIGHTHAWK PRESS
TAOS, NEW MEXICO

My Brooklyn Bridge: Take a Journey with Me as I Build a Career in Dentistry, Inventing, and Furnature. Copyright © 2024 by Jeffrey M. Hills. All rights reserved. Printed in the United States of America. No part of this book may be used or reproduced in any manner whatsoever without written permission, other than in the case of brief quotations embodied in critical articles and reviews. For information address: Nighthawk Press, PO Box 1222, Taos NM 87571.

—

FIRST EDITION 2024

—

My Brooklyn Bridge: Take a Journey with Me as I Build a Career
in Dentistry, Inventing, and Furnature / Jeffrey M. Hills

Hills, Jeffrey (December 12, 1946 –)

Published by Nighthawk Press, Taos, New Mexico
Cover and book design by Kelly Pasholk, Wink Visual Arts

Cover background photo of Walnut table built and photographed by Jeffrey Hills
Front cover photo of Jeffrey's hands by Phyllis Hills
Photo of Brooklyn Bridge, page 2, by Timothy Penso
Photo of Havasu Falls, page 46, by Jeffrey M. Hills
Photo of Jeffrey Hills Hands, page 132, by Phyllis Hills
Photos of Hills Group, page 163, by Gilbert Mares
Photos of Brett Hills Skiing, page 167, by Kevin Rebholtz
Photo of Jeffrey, Phyllis, Olivia, Sam, and Airstream, page 180, by Rachael Shaheen
Miscellaneous photos throughout the book by Phyllis Hills, Jeffrey Hills, and Brett Hills
Conoid Chairs, pages 79 and 138, inspired by George Nakashima

Library of Congress Control Number: 2024912203
ISBN: 979-8-9888976-1-3

To my wife Phyllis

Wife, Friend and Muse . . . tireless, courageous, loving

To my Grandchildren

Olivia and Sam

We have given you stories to tell, memories to share

CONTENTS

Foreword   ix

PART I   1

1   Brooklyn and Beyond
Take Me Out to the Ball Game; Take Me Out West   3

2   Early Teens—Reflections on a Book
Remembering and Revering a First Book   7

3   Montreal Expo 1967, Mount Washington 1975
Two Friends, Two Adventures   9

4   Failure—The Long Way Around to Success
Failure Is Success Turned Inside Out   15

5   Paying It Forward Before It Was Paying It Forward
The Zen of What Goes Around Comes Around   19

6   Moab
Sand and Water Entrap Us Twice   21

7   Dental Practice
Dentistry—Dental Career
Education, Innovation, Customer Service   29

8   One Door, Two Houses, and the Long Way Home   33

9   A Home Defined
The Hope of Solar and Science   37

10   The Triathlon
Two Birds, One Stone   41

11   Lake Powell and Havasu Falls
The Blue Green Water and the Four Horses of Havasu   47

12   In Days Gone By
The Way We Were   51

13	France	53
14	One Boat, Two Adventures The Sea Calls for Seamanship	57
15	Crossing Paths Again Edward Abbey, Naturalist, Conservationist	65
16	The Motor Vessel David B On the Water, Where I Long to Be	67
17	A Horse Named Charlie A Dear Friend Named Larry	73
18	A Special Museum Leads to a Special Visit The Tables Are Turned	77
19	For the Fun of Cars The Automobile Joining Design and Engineering	85
20	Today	97

Part II   101

Patent Number 3,722,020   103

Part III   131

Las Manos del Hombre
Woodworking   133

Part IV   157

Photo Album—Family and Friends   158

Thank You   175

About the Author   177

FOREWORD

I was born in Brooklyn, New York on December 12, 1946. I am told it was a cloudy December day. When I was very young, five or six, I was gifted a paint by number canvas of the Brooklyn Bridge. I remember enjoying the delicate hand to brush, paint to canvas experience, which I have enjoyed in many of my endeavors particularly Dentistry and Woodworking, and written about extensively in this book.

"Brooklyn and Beyond" is not only the first chapter, it also seems to me, in reflection, to be a developmental cornerstone of my life. Certainly an identity that I cherish and welcome into any conversation that begins with, "where are you from?" My title pays homage to my birth place, childhood and my first "art."

A circle represents one story. The intersecting circles of the Olympic logo represent the amalgamation of stories. This compilation of my stories, even though all bound together neatly and tidily between the front cover and the back cover, is how the process of my writing took place.

Over the last decade I have kept track of my favorite stories that I have told. I have also thought deeply about what endeavors have meant the most to me, both in my mind and in my heart. Put another way, imagine I am in hospice and my Grandchildren come to visit me for the day. They say, "PopPop, tell us some of your favorite stories, we would love to hear them." I would want to entertain as I love, with humor and irony. I would also want to convey who I was, the life I have lived, the legacy I want to go forward to the next generation.

It would be convenient if life and these stories were as simple as peeling an onion, layer by layer. But that is not reality. Some stories are hours to one day events. The duration does not diminish the importance. At the extreme, some of the stories are a year, decade, even life times in the making. This long duration does not give these stories "super powers." In essence life is unfolding in a very complex overlapping of circles or arcs. For example, in the 1970s on any given day I would wake up, shower and practice Dentistry. Simple and straight forward. However, I may train for my fourth coming triathlon by running before that shower, swimming at lunch break and taking a bike ride before dinner. I may talk with the builder of our new home and also touch base with my patent attorney for my new invention. In other words, think of circles, small and large representing my day, my week and so forth. Many of these circles intersect and overlap simultaneously.

For clarity and continuity I have unraveled each story and disengaged it from a linear orderly day, thereby allowing each story to stand on its own uncluttered, unengaged merits. A notable exception to this style is "Mengie a Special Museum Visit," which has multiple flash backs, by necessity.

The stories share two main themes, work and play. Play is often represented by some adventure, often going sideways.

The common theme of work includes creativity and how to nurture one's intuitiveness in the creative process.

Another theme is how to design, to tap into both form and function. In the next step a sense of how to work as an inventor and a craftsman.

Lastly, the power of integrity and ethics in one's work. These themes are continually represented in my many stories.

As much as possible there is a chronological order to these stories, either by first date of onset or by their "true arc" in my life. For example, "Las Manos del Hombre," the story of my career as a furniture maker, had many firsts and achievements in the 50s, 60s and 70s. By the 80s my exceptional growth of talent and consistently fine work and then professional recognition began to occur. I chose therefore the 80s to place the story, yet it is clear that the beginnings were much earlier and my Gallery experience most currently significant and ongoing.

One can read and enjoy these stories as special and individual experiences to be enjoyed as such. One can also use the Table of Contents as a guide for the appreciation of intersecting and the over lapping sense of time and experience. In other words, these personal snapshots of my life can be simply enjoyed or more complexly experienced.

I am both honored and grateful to share my life with you.

Part I

1 1950s

BROOKLYN AND BEYOND
Take Me Out to the Ball Game; Take Me Out West

"How lucky to be born in Brooklyn in 1946."

— *When Brooklyn was the World, 1920-1957,* a book
   by Elliot Wilensky.

Brooklyn: A borough of New York City, of about three million residents, with three of its borders defined by water. To the south is Brighton Beach and Coney Island. In 1920, my father was born in Brooklyn; my Mother was born a year later. They both went to Tilden High School and married in 1940. My Father enlisted in the Army when World War II broke out. My Mother worked as a secretary for Naval operations at the Bushwick Naval Center, in Brooklyn.

Growing up I would go to Brighton Beach Baths with my Father who was an avid handball player. The zenith of his handball competition was to play in Center Court in Brighton Beach. I do remember the crowd in the stands but I cannot recall the outcome of the championship match, maybe for the better.

I do recall walking alongside the huge swimming pool when all of a sudden someone pushed me, this five-year-old or so nonswimmer, in! OK, sink or swim; for this five-year-old, it was swim. After all, I was from Brooklyn.

Summer nights and Coney Island were the best. Bumper cars followed by a Nathan's hot dog and a drink served in a Nathan's glass for ten cents additional.

Brooklyn was really about two things, your neighborhood and your Brooklyn Dodgers.

The neighborhood had it all, a bakery, delicatessen, two candy stores, a butcher, and produce stores complete with pickle barrels, yum and no hygiene needed: you could just throw your arm in to grab a pickle. The candy stores had any candy you could want and gum, especially Bazooka with baseball players cards in the wrapper. If you had ten cents you could get a soda pop out of the ice cooler on the sidewalk outside, with red and white Coca-Cola written on the front. If you had a quarter you could sit at the counter and enjoy a malted milk shake or an ice cream soda float. My Father's cousin had a candy store in Williamsburg. He would make me a fried egg on a freshly buttered kaiser roll. I can still taste it. Every sort of outside game and activity you could imagine, stoop ball, pink ball, hand ball, stick ball, caps, box ball, every sort of rope jumping—what a time, what sweet memories.

The Brooklyn Dodgers played Baseball in Ebbets Field, a small stadium built on one block and surrounded by a neighborhood.

My dad took me to my first Dodgers game, where a Jewish Hall of Famer, Sandy Koufax, pitched a shutout game, which to my seven-year-old self seemed "oh so boring." No crazy base running or home runs to cheer over. The Dodgers were perennial also-rans; they could get to the World Series, they just could not win the World Series. They left the winning to the New York Yankees. All so disappointing and frustrating until 1955. The October Classic, game seven against the Yankees, ended with Johnny Podres pitching a victory and Brooklyn exploded. After decades of frustration and "wait till next year," Brooklyn hosted a mammoth block party. I can remember running wildly down the block and at the top of my lungs yelling "We won! We won!" over and over, and that is also the logic my father used in adopting "55" as his lucky number. Thinking back, it had a nice ring to it and it sure beats losing. What came next was losing in 1956 to the Yankees and Don Larsen's perfect game. At least I got to see Yogi Berra jump on Larsen after the final out. Yogi was one of a kind. A good player, a good man, and one special kind of "nut." Who else could say, "It's *déja vu* all over again," or "If you see a fork in the road, take it," and be both humorously and seriously taken?

In 1957, owner Walter O'Malley moved his Brooklyn Dodgers to Los Angeles, California. Unthinkable, unimaginable to a ten-year-old, incomprehensible! By now we had lived on Long Island for two years but we still got to see games at Ebbets Field with parental help. With the Dodgers gone what was the point?

When Brooklyn was the world, it ended in 1957, no small coincidence.

Life on Long Island, especially in the bland middle, and its bland suburbs was made enjoyable by my many friends who were into sports play and outside activities. As a matter of course, we all went off to college and we went our separate ways.

My best friend, Peter Dolgoff, took off as well, although we did cross paths at Hofstra University. Then I was off to Dental School and Peter was off to life. At Hofstra we picked up where we left off with street hockey. We played roller hockey and Hofstra club ice hockey. We lost touch for years and then reconnected and remain best of friends today.

A high school acquaintance, Larry Schreiber, who had followed in his brother's footsteps and had enrolled in the Citadel Military College in South Carolina, decided in his first semester that a military school was not for him. He dropped out and came home for some R & R. After enrolling in Hofstra College, he knew I was there, and he gave me a call.

We would often be taking the same science programs either in the same class or with the same professor. The notion of studying together in the evening was both practical and motivating for the both of us. In late winter of our senior year, our applications to our various schools were submitted. The medical and dental schools would send out their letters on about the same week in April.

When I received my letter of acceptance from Temple University in Philadelphia I hit the roof with joy. After four years of hard work in college and a deferment from Vietnam, I hit the lottery. With joy and trepidation I called Larry. "I got accepted, did you hear?"—"Yes, two days ago!"—"Why didn't you tell me?"—He answered, "I knew you hadn't heard yet!" A compassionate friend, Dr. Larry Schreiber went on to be the definition of an outstanding and compassionate physician or his Taos community.

On our many visits to New Mexico, we enjoyed a visit to Larry and his growing family. From time to time he was my dental patient and I was his medical patient. Our son Brett considered Larry his "godfather" and after college he settled in Taos to work, ski ,and be near his godfather, for parental support if he should need it.

Our many visits to Taos, with its active art scene and a multicultural population, and with our son in Albuquerque, our retirement location in Taos was a natural. Our daughter Rachael's family with our two grandchildren, Olivia and Samuel, live just five hours north, outside of Denver, Colorado.

2 1950s

EARLY TEENS
REFLECTIONS ON A BOOK
Remembering and Revering a First Book

*Lying in bed one night, while reading a
library book I paused ...*

I realized there weren't books in my childhood home! I would borrow from the Library.

First Books: Borrowed and returned to the Library.

As I recall I took books out on baseball, football, race cars, car mechanics, car repairs, woodworking and tools.

Then one Thanksgiving my older cousin Michael took me to his room and gave me books on nursery rhymes to keep. He saw my awe and joy. A book of my own. He shortly thereafter gave me a book that came to define myself and my life. *The Book of Wonder,* the building of bridges, sky scrapers, dams, tunnels and how these and other big projects were engineered and built.

It was brand new and mine, my first book. I read it over and over and then when I was about ten years old I started to build things—a foot stool, a frame, a toy. Then all sorts of things for friends, for play, for my Mom, for my Dad. Although I was an academic and science student in East Meadow High School, shop class—wood and metal work, was a requirement. Graduation came at last. At the senior awards assembly I was shocked to hear my name called out as the New York State

Steering Commission Award recipient (Excellence in Industrial Arts). My work was perfect in every detail. All the Industrial Arts students were as amazed as I was. I later gave the award, which was a pin, to my future wife Phyllis.

I went on to study and became a Dentist. I invented a toothbrush cited over 70 times worldwide and used by millions. I built furniture for our three homes, for my children and grandchildren. I have been published numerous times and awarded the distinction of "Taos Living Master." Collectors have purchased my work worldwide and I built and designed eight homes along the way.

The Book of Wonder did more than satisfy my curiosity, and it taught me that the wonder was in the inspiration, feeling the fire in my belly, and the experience of passion in my heart.

I recently built for our home speaker stands, so simple but yet so complex and elegant. Neither drawing attention to nor diverting the eye, simply and beautifully present with harmony of the whole. Every line, curved or angled, defined quiet elegance. I look at these elegant speaker stands and think back to over 65 years of becoming a craftsman and I say to myself, "Who would have thought I could have done this?"

I still find joy and such personal satisfaction in my craft, my hands as learned.

The amazement and fascination of it all. *The Book of Wonder* was but a book, a wonderful book and a gift of, and for, a life time of purpose, passion and joy.

3   1967
         1975

MONTREAL EXPO 1967
MOUNT WASHINGTON 1975
Two Friends, Two Adventures

Montreal Expo 1967

Mike Ehrenpreis and I met when we were about eleven, while at the same day camp out on Long Island. We became fast friends over the summer but by fall we realized that we lived a few towns apart. At this distance and given our age, our friendship would not be served well.

Years later, as I began college at Hofstra University on Long Island, I was startled and pleased to run into Mike again. He was tall, trim, and quick with a joke or a song. He sang standards with a lovely tenor voice. We seemed to always be in different classes but we would meet at Memorial Hall for lunch. Somewhere along the line we decided to take his Uncle's and Father's Chris-Craft 23' boat, The Budd III, to Montreal Expo '67. After convincing our parents and provisioning the boat with beer, canned food, and more beer, along with some maps, we picked up Kenny, a mutual friend to make it a crew of three on board. We decided we would finish up our summer work and squeeze the trip in before the fall semester.

Late summer 1967 we left our dock in Bellmore, Long Island, and headed out to the Atlantic Ocean. We ran parallel to Queens and Brooklyn until we reached the Verrazano Narrows, then made a turn to starboard and cruised under the new (1964) Verrazano Bridge, a near mile-long suspension bridge connecting Brooklyn to Staten

Island. The Statue of Liberty gleaming in the sunlight to port and lower Manhattan straight ahead. The World Trade Towers would not be complete for another five years.

We navigated up the Hudson River going under the bridges, one by one. In Poughkeepsie, New York, the water transitioned from brackish to fresh, free of salination. The next few hours brought us to the New York State Barge Canal. This would raise us hundreds of feet to Lake Champlain. The sun was setting over the mirror-like waters of the lake, the boat on a delightful plane, as the fall foliage reflected the bright oranges, reds, and yellows off the water. Mike hit the throttle and we cruised under full power into Essex, New York. We tied up, befriended a nice black marina dog, had a canned dinner and drifted off to sleep.

The sun rose and we were off to Rouses Point, customs, and entry to Canada.

As a courtesy we replaced our ensign (American flag) with that of Canada. We were now on the River Richelieu, flowing with us south to north. A day spent cruising at hull speed (approximately 6 knots, with no wake) going lock to lock. The Canadian locks which had large steel doors on both ends, were managed by two burly men on opposite sides of the large horizontal wheel.

On the entry and exit side of each lock was a long wharf we could tie up to for the night. That is exactly what we did. Once again, a beer induced sleep had come to us. However, an unusual sound broke through our slumber.

What was that gurgling sound? It was water rising over the deck, not good! We pulled the engine hatch.

There was a rubber hose split and gushing water, which looked to be below sea level. "Holy cow, we have a problem." Yes we do! OK, we are sinking. The trouble was here, a burst hose, the adventure had started.

I pulled out the packs of gum we had and shouted, "Chew as much as you can as fast as you can." I found the black plastic electrical tape, mashed all the chewed gum into a wad. I slapped the wad of gum over the gash and wrapped the gum tightly around the hose with the electrical tape. The automatic PAR water pump had been going but now it was beginning to make headway. We sent Kenny to the lockkeepers' house for help. One did not speak French and the other did not speak English, so to no avail. Fortunately we were doing better with the Juicy Fruit gum and tape.

The real test would come the next morning when we started the engine and put the repair under load. It held! So we continued north to the city of Sorrel at the juncture of the River Richelieu and the St. Lawrence River. We entered the St. Lawrence, turned to port, and a few hours later found our marina in Montreal. We made arrangements to have the boat hauled and repairs made.

> The real test would come the next morning

After enjoying the sights and Beer Gardens of Expo '67 we were homeward bound. To this day, every car and boat I have provisioned has chewing gum and electrical tape. Of course I have never needed those items again. Many years later Mike gifted me the nautical chart of Montreal and the compass from the boat. Saving a friend's boat, which was really his father's and uncle's boat, can be a pretty big deal, at least for that friend.

1975

Mount Washington Late Winter

Mike and I had another great idea, let's climb Mt. Washington in New Hampshire under winter conditions.

First some perspective on the data for Mt. Washington:

1. The record low... -50 degrees °F
2. The highest recorded wind speed... 231 mph
3. The lowest recorded wind chill... -108 degrees
4. It can snow August through June... 11 months

I picked Mike up in Manhattan, one cold and rainy evening, all gear was packed in and we were off to North Conway, New Hampshire. We slept at the youth hostel there and woke to a full breakfast, which was a great way to fuel up for the climb ahead.

In the parking lot we found my Fjord Blue 2002 tii BMW sports sedan and geared up. Warm layers, hiking boots, water, food, and of all things, crampons (spiked iron plates to be worn over boots for traction on snow and ice), and an ice axe. The ice axe aids in walking on icy surfaces, climbing and even going up a vertical ice wall. A spoon-shaped end can be used to dig an emergency shelter. The ice axe was officially brought to America by a couple who were part of a Northwest (Seattle) climbing group. They ordered the ice axe from Australia at a cost of $3 each. With other climbing gear brought in they started a co-op in 1938. This co-op became REI, which I joined in the mid 1970s. I bought this same wood handled ice axe from Australia. It is today signed and hanging in my son's sports bar at his home. The ice ax started it all for REI, according to their history. Many of their retail stores use this ice axe for their entrance door handles.

So we set out, a rather casual climb, along with skiers who were headed up to Tuckerman's Ravine. The skiers hike up to do one steep run and they are done. Technically, Tuckerman's Ravine is up to a 55 degree pitch. The complete run comes in at four thousand feet. The hike up Lion's Head is steeper and more rugged—yes time for the ice axe and crampons. It was sunny and the temperatures were accommodating, with magnificent views. We reached the peak; now how to get down. Time for "glissade!" In a sitting position, heels dug in for steering and speed control. The ice axe held close to the body, dug into the snow to act as a rudder and for help in braking. The only problem, you cannot practice this in Philadelphia or Manhattan. It was baptism by fire and stay away from boulders for sure. Fifty years later my most vivid memory was just how fast it was to get down, especially after hours of climbing up! We made it down snow covered and in one piece. From there it was an easy trail walk to the hostel and a great dinner of comfort food. The hardest part was the respect needed for the mountain, the potential weather, proper gear ,and (even if unable to practice too much beforehand) proper mountain techniques. I did not have a bucket list back then, but if I had, then a Mount Washington assent on snow and ice would be in the bucket.

A little over a month later our daughter Rachael was born.

4 1966

FAILURE
THE LONG WAY AROUND TO SUCCESS
Failure Is Success Turned Inside Out

Stunned, literally breathless. My first quiz in college summer school—organic chemistry, sitting on my desk—at the top of the graded paper: 16! It was not 16 out of 20, but 16 out of 100! The usual way testing numbers work.

My hopes for applying and being accepted to dental school flashed before me as a bleak hope, in fact very bleak.

Dental school required Organic Chemistry as a core course of study for admission, fair enough. I knew Organic Chemistry 101 was not going to be my jam, so in order to get a bit of an edge, why not take it in summer school? I would have to focus on and study only one subject. Six weeks later I would be done. Dr. Di Angelo was a graduate level professor, teaching a basic 101 level course. He obviously saw it differently. Although the book was standard issue, the course was compressed into six weeks. The real crux was the testing, which was over my head. It didn't much matter how hard I studied, I was not an Organic Chemistry master. Well, a grade of 16, maybe I will catch on, get the handle on it. I did improve by 100% on the next quiz, a 32, yes out of 100.

This was not going to get me into dental school. You may have heard there was a war with a real draft going on—the Vietnam War.

With one week to go and one final exam to go, Dr. Di Angelo called me into his office. He was pleasant enough, with horned rimmed glasses and a tweed coat, very scholarly. He said, "I know you are working hard, maybe the pace in summer school is too fast." He continued, "You can tough it out but will likely get an F or you can drop the course and I will submit an incomplete." He offered, "You can take the course during the regular semester next year."

Six weeks of constant work and the worst part, I had tickets to see Barbra Streisand at Forest Hills Tennis Stadium, Center Court. I had to give them to a friend to take my girl friend (future and current wife) to enjoy the concert while I studied for the midterm exam.

The choice of an incomplete was still the best of all options. I dropped the course and took it again in the fall. The slowed down version helped and I was taught by the professor whom I knew from Inorganic Chemistry. We got along well and I earned a B. It may have been the long way around but it was a path that led me to a dental school acceptance.

> # Failure is just success inside out.

It is said that failure is just one hundred and eighty degrees from success or that success is failure turned inside out.

I see it as an emotional experience as well. You are upset, discouraged and essentially grieving a loss. So how and why do some recover, pick themselves up, dust themselves off and start all over again, while others quit?

Early in my sophomore year of dental school, through a moment of inspiration, I experienced an aha moment. It is called the moment of invention.

The moment and credit of that one moment of creativity would last a life time. It was, however, a two-edged sword. Success and Failure. My idea succeeded beyond my wildest dreams, but the recognition due me—not so much. Any financial gain was more than offset by exceedingly long hours of work, plus large amounts of out-of-pocket money needed to feed the "beast," the Invention.

The idea first came to life in the fall of 1969 during a dental school class lecture on tooth brushing. Patent pending and the utility patent protected the mechanical design for twenty-one years until March 27, 1990. Seemingly a day later Procter & Gamble came out with their version. Although a design patent only, still it necessitated the citation of my Utility Patent, which was now in the public domain. It has since been cited over 72 times throughout the world, and still counting.

Emotional intelligence and the ability to find the positive in it or find a new positive, while life and time marches on was a challenge. There were mouths to feed, debts to be paid, and most of all I had my dental degree and the ability, skill set, and license to practice dentistry, my career choice.

The toothbrush was not a failure, but it was failing to find a manufacturer and the machinery to manufacture the brush. As I moved forward I realized that failure could not exist alongside success. There is simply not enough space for the two. Success carries so many positive emotions, joy to mention one. Joy, in and of itself, is a powerful counter weight to defeat. As the saying goes, "You can't win them all, but hope springs eternal." We do not get to choose when we have good luck or bad luck. In spite of our best efforts and hard work, success is not guaranteed. However, we do get to have the maturity and wisdom to accept, process, and move on.

There is often another project or challenge around the corner, but you must choose to turn and round that corner. The satisfaction of a successful creative effort is ultimately measured in emotional joy. However much deserved and earned, financial reward is another measure of the successful creative project.

I go back to my favorite high school novel, the 1925 medical story, *Arrowsmith,* by Sinclair Lewis. The closing is particularly noteworthy. "I feel as if we were really beginning to work now, said Martin. This new Quinine stuff may prove pretty good. We'll plug along on it for two or three years, and maybe we will get something permanent—and probably we'll fail." Thus ends the novel. Somehow it does not seem to matter if they fail, for the truth is in the search and the faith that one day they may find something. And at least, he has been true to himself. Patience and Perseverance in service of Purpose.

Patience and Perseverance in service of Purpose.

5   1972
1986

PAYING IT FORWARD
BEFORE IT WAS PAYING IT FORWARD
The Zen of What Goes Around Comes Around

In 1972, while driving the FJ40, all boxy, bouncy, and blue, with infant son out west, we were on our way to Bryce Canyon National Park. We could take the highway or an old logging road. Since I was driving an FJ40 you know what road I would choose, so the dirt road it was. We had to travel at a speed that would at least get us there in day light. The FJ40 met a crater in the road and we went airborne. When we landed our rooftop carrier had come down thirty feet behind us. A huge mess of baby bottles, formula and diapers. But first to repair and reattach the rooftop carrier. Grateful for spare parts and hardware and about an hour later we were on our way. When we arrived at our camp site we were filthy, but worse yet, all the bottles to feed Brett were dirty as well. Phyllis tended to Brett and I washed and cleaned the bottles. I was feeling a bit sorry for myself when I looked up to see an older man holding a plate with a sizzling steak on it. I will never forget his words, "Looks like you could use a nice steak." Yes indeed I could, and it would indeed be one I would never forget!

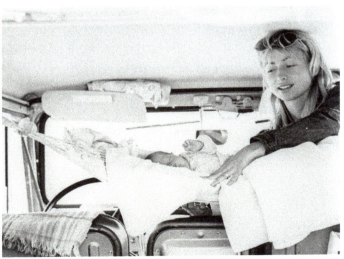

That was the early 1970s. By the mid 1980s we had our houseboat, a forty-six foot junker with of course my BMW Alpine sound system on Lake Powell. One night we were tied up in a quiet cove. It was not quiet for long. An August storm had picked up and sheets of rain were coming down. Other than a noisy night we stayed dry. When we woke up we saw a boat buried in sand and mud up to the rails on the other side of the cove. We could make out an adult man and a woman and a large group of kids. While they were digging out I dug into our food stores. Scrambled up a dozen eggs, pulled out a loaf of bread and volunteered Brett to deliver breakfast to this family. They did not realize that they had beached their boat at the mouth of a wash. It actually could have been worse, more sand and less eggs.

There are many examples we all can recall of acts of kindness. Sometimes we receive and sometimes we give, but always grateful for the opportunity to play either side.

I have always been happy with our decision, Phyllis and myself along with our son, to establish the Presbyterian Hills Family Foundation for Cancer Care.

I have always been happy with our decision, Phyllis and myself along with our son, to establish the Presbyterian Hills Family Foundation for Cancer Care in Albuquerque. This is in honor of Phyllis being a cancer survivor for over twenty years. The Foundation supports medical personnel in their continuing education programs at MD Anderson Medical Center in Houston. It also helps provide transportation for outpatients undergoing chemotherapy or radiation therapy. Paying back is giving thanks and gratitude. We have taken a stake in our communities health care and it is of no coincidence to me that on a tough day as a young parent, someone cooked up a steak to care for me, and inspire my appetite for paying it forward.

6 1973-2017

MOAB 1973, 1983, 2013
SAND AND WATER ENTRAP US TWICE
Early 70s, early 80s, and More

The story of Moab Canyonlands National Park begins in July of 1973. To truly appreciate it, we start our story on Lake Powell, fall of 2013, and then flash back. We had just bought a 22-foot, 2000 Chapparral IO with our son Brett.

We trailered the boat from Taos to Lake Powell for its maiden trip and outing. Of course the typical seasonal monsoon weather, cloudy, hot, and threatening, was to be expected. We put in at Wahweap Bay, as we were heading out to spend the night on a nearby beach. The weather began to close in, even darker and more threatening. It was

time to seek a protected shelter and hunker down. I was looking for a leeward shore to beach the boat safely from the storm coming in from the east. The Saturday afternoon crowd left me with only windward shore choices. After beaching and raising the stern outdrive, I set out a port and starboard anchor on the beach. We were stable and secure. The wind kicked up, but we were still rain free. While our dog Duke was exploring the area I built a fire in a hole I dug in the sand, over which I would later place a grill and cook up some dinner. A good plan until it wasn't. Just then a few young woman passed by asking me if I knew where to find some firewood? I reminded them that this was a desert, save for the Lake. I also offered them some of the firewood I had brought with me, as I had more than enough. They thanked me and went on their way. A short while later they returned empty handed and asked if they could take me up on "that wood offer," I obliged and soon after the rains began. Without a hot meal to enjoy we did the next best thing, made two gin and tonics for dinner and two more for desert. Even though the storm raged we slept till first light. I became aware that the boat was not rocking and thumping any longer. In a snap, I was out into the warm water, with the sun rising, and upon inspection, to my horror, the hull was buried in the sand! The windward shore was not looking as good a choice as I had hoped. I grabbed my goggles and shovel and went to work. About three hours later I had pulled a sandy trough away from the hull and transom. Still, the boat would not move an inch. Sand under the boat as well as the adhesive nature of water were the issues. Due to the shallow water depth I could not lower the stern drive and power us off. I needed help and lots of it.

Phyllis went down the beach to the houseboat where the "firewood" women were staying. Happily they remembered me and my gift of firewood and said they would be right along. Ten minutes later I looked and with delight and relief I saw twelve beautiful folks, some with shovels, walking toward our "stuck boat." What a welcome sight! We did a little more digging to free a path for the stern to push into deeper water, and just before we organized for the big push, one of the younger women announced, "my boy friend always says, the adventure doesn't start until you get in trouble," That is some solid outdoor wisdom! Fortunately I had a crew to extricate us out of trouble.

With about seven of us on the port and seven on the starboard, a minute or two of grunting led to a loud cheer, while I ran into the water to chase down the boat, climb aboard and get the engine started so I could lightly rebeach the bow and pick up Phyllis and Duke. We then went out a bit into deeper water and set the anchor. We had some cold breakfast, which was needed and delicious.

Duke started to sniff around letting us know he had a need to go ashore for a "business" meeting. I dove in the water and he jumped in right behind me. Side by side we swam to shore where terra firma welcomed him and his "business" (which I cleaned up and buried deeply). Shortly we swam back to the boat together. He grabbed the swim platform with his front paws, I grabbed his collar and pulled up and in he was.

Let's flash back to 1973, our motorcycle trip out west. We were riding a BMW 600/5, black with a large wind screen. Our friends Beth and Kent were on a BMW 700/5. Cruising from Philadelphia to points west. Arizona, Utah, New Mexico,and Colorado. In Utah we decided to visit Canyonlands National Park, which was established in 1964.

We rented a beat up 4X4 Chevy Blazer in the nearby town of Moab, and after an hour's drive we began exploring. We decided to stay in the park at a place called Canyonlands Resort, which was nothing more than a group of trailers on four wheels. After looking at the guide book, a plan was made. We would head out early before the July heat set in, small back packs and a half gallon of water each, in a traditional blanketed canteen. There were no camelbacks or energy bars in those days. We would drive south to the Needles district then traverse Elephant Hill, a ridiculously steep "mountain" of slick rock and boulders. Over Elephant Hill, a class IV jeep trail, to upper Red Lake Canyon. Then leaving the 4X4 Blazer behind on the double track, we would hike on the single track to lower Red Lake Canyon all the way to the Colorado River, approximately two miles.

We headed out in our rented 4X4 Chevy Blazer, beat up from scraping the canyon walls. First destination and surprise, the Elephant Hill 4X4 trail. The National Park Service describes it as follows, "One of the most technical four wheel drive roads in Utah, Elephant Hill presents drivers with steep grades, loose rock, stair step drops, tight turns and tricky backing. Once over the Hill, equally challenging roads lead to various features and hiking trails to the Colorado River."

With Kent driving it was early and we were doing well, at least until we weren't. The Blazer was not steering properly and an inspection was called for. Kent was a superb mechanic, who could take apart an engine and put it back together without missing a beat. My specialty, navigation with real road maps. Speed, time, and

distance calculations all done in my head while riding at 65 mph or thereabouts. As well, I could put a provision list together in a snap.

Kent found that the steering box had worked loose. Short of tools and hardware his only choice was to harvest some bolts from another part of the Blazer, with what few tools we had.

With that done and valuable time lost, we set out again to complete the notorious Elephant Hill Jeep Trail. The steering was steady but the temperature was rising fast. We pulled over where upper Red Lake Canyon, a double track met the single track of lower Red Lake Canyon. It soon became obvious that we were in the heat of the day. The July heat was now dictating our schedule. We were to hike to the Colorado River and perhaps take a cooling dip. At the half way point our thirst was great and our water supply was not. Looking at our arms covered in the desert dust you could see hundreds of dots, tiny clear dots. Sweating and evaporation in the desert heat are almost simultaneous. There is no wet film on your brow or arm, only dots. Edward Abbey writes in his survival book, Desert Solitaire, "The best place to store water is in your stomach." That horse had already left the barn. First choice, turn back. We did not think we could make it physically or have enough hydration. Second choice, make it to the River and refill our canteens. We decided to leave the wives to take shelter under a rock that provided shade. They would share one canteen.

Kent and I trekked down further to the River. If you can see trees and vegetation that is a good sign you are nearing water. Our goal was in sight. There was however, something we could not know, regardless of how close we got. Finally, as exhaustion was setting in and heat stroke was approaching, a pool of water appeared. Kent took all three of the canteens and jumped into the cool water. It quickly became apparent there was a problem. While filling the canteens he screamed, "Help, I am stuck in quick sand." I searched for a long branch to extend to him and luckily I could reach his outstretched hand and pull him and the water he carried to shore. He was wasted and spent but we had water. The water had twigs and live bugs in it, which was a good sign according to Abbey. It indicated that it was good water with no arsenic in it. We hiked up the trail and drank sparingly. The insistent heat was now surpassed by Kent's affliction with more and more episodes of diarrhea. By the time we reached the girls, who had no idea of the sudden turn of events, it was clear Kent's hike was over. Interestingly, neither of the three of us got sick drinking the same water, which leads me to believe Kent had his own bug or the onset of hyperthermia.

Phyllis and I hiked back to the 4X4 Blazer. Having grown up and driven on the flat roads of Long Island, it was time to tackle the class IV degree of difficulty, Elephant Hill, back to the Ranger Station for help. Baptism by fire for sure.

I knew how to shift, but not so easy pitched at forty five degrees. This was no time to stall out. One would need one foot on the brake, one on the clutch and one on the gas. But you may ask, who has three feet?

The proper technique:

Foot on the brake

Turn engine key on, neutral gear, clutch in

Foot off the brake and clutch pedal

Roll in reverse

Shift to reverse

Pop clutch out

Engine roars to life

Pop clutch in

Foot on brake

Shift to first

Right foot on gas

Engage clutch slowly

Pull forward slowly and do not stall out.

Also, when rolling backwards, do not roll over the edge, there are no guard rails, only a thousand foot drop!

We made it to the ranger station and while the sun was setting we explained the problem to the rangers. They said, "Well it will take about an hour to get ready." They gathered water, first aid supplies, and a litter basket for on trail portage. All the covers were off the gas pumps, exposing the pump with all its pipes. The rangers explained to me the problem of vapor locking, where gas can not flow because the vapors have locked up to cause a blockage. In order to get around this they sprayed a stream of water on the exposed pipes to cool the gas and reduce the vapors and pump slowly. A half hour later we had fuel and I was informed that I was going back over Elephant Hill with the rangers to find my friend. It was eerie at night in the dark with the lights playing off the rocky sandstone walls.

We found Beth and Kent with a group of young teens coming off the trail. Fresh water, cooler temperatures and the time to rest settled him down for the trip home by flashlight. We loaded them into the 4X4 and, yep, back over Elephant Hill. When we got back to the ranger station, the lead ranger said, "See me first thing in the morning,"

We had a few beers and a few laughs to go with our microwave dinner and sleep came easily. The next morning we met up with the rescue ranger. He was none too happy with us, as I caught him just as he was to go off duty and probably do a cold six pack the afternoon before.

All grizzly and snarly he said, "See that book over there, buy it, read it, twice if you have to. Then you can come back to my Park." I read it and returned at least twelve more times for my adventures in Canyonlands. I've hiked it, jeeped it in a 4X4, and flown over it. Hiked to the Confluence, logged 110 miles of Rim Road. I've done solo Jeep trips and soloed over Elephant Hill. The quietness, expanse, and beauty, has left me breathless with awe and psychologically refreshed time after time.

OK, the book the ranger told me to buy, *Desert Solitaire, A Season in the Wilderness,* by Edward Abbey, which chronicled his time in the late 1960s as Park Superintendent for Arches National Monument, which is right across highway 191. (It was not yet a designated National Park). While telling his story he also teaches desert survival. Water is scarce until it is too abundant; flash floods occur. It is dry and hot in the summer; there are some springs, mostly hidden and some may be laden with salt, arsenic, or both. Fresh water comes with the bugs and the algae on the surface. The not so fresh will soon introduce you to the circling vultures above. He teaches that water will make sand gooey, better known as quick sand. Deadly to cattle and entrapping to man. Lay down for more surface area to buoy you up, or get pulled out. August and September brings sudden cloudbursts up stream, torrents of quick rain and miles away your sunny dry canyon will soon be a wall of water, sand, mud, and small trees; you will be face to face with a flash flood. It can kill or trap all in its path. Know your weather, especially up stream, and plan accordingly.

Dare to hike in July and dare to know heat stroke and hyperthermia, which will put you in danger. Only decisive action will save you; your body is cooking. Have plenty of water, avoid the heat of the day, dress accordingly, and do not trail cut (between switch backs).

When we got in trouble on the Elephant Hill trail, it followed a typical disaster pattern. Dominoes falling. First one thing and then another. Planning and preparation are crucial. We should have carried two canteens each or one gallon of water each. When we got delayed with the steering box break down, we could have done a shorter trip and adjusted the plan accordingly. Once again, the young woman on Lake Powell had it right. It is not an adventure until the trouble starts. Only this time the stakes were life itself.

7 1972

DENTAL PRACTICE
DENTISTRY–DENTAL CAREER
Education, Innovation, Customer Service

During my senior year of dental school I finished my clinical requirements early, which enabled me to be a rotating student intern in the Periodontal and Endodontic Departments. It was a terrific opportunity to get advanced education and practice in these two fields.

I was also doing advanced work in Restorative Dentistry and Prosthetics, with Professor Dr. Peter Costa who would employ me as a dentist on his staff in his Villanova, Pennsylvania, office.

At the beginning of my sophomore year Phyllis and I married and I had invented my toothbrush. I was looking for a twenty-six hour day, but to no avail. There was never enough time between studies, clinic patients, and the toothbrush. I think I am still catching up on sleep. By graduation our son Brett was born. Although I had already taken the dental board examinations, I would not be licensed to practice until August, 1972. With time to kill, we outfitted our Toyota FJ40 Land Cruiser, a very stiff and crude version of today's all wheel drive SUV, and set out for Albuquerque, New Mexico, home to our two friends Larry and Carol Schreiber. The trip to Albuquerque was an adventure with a dog and a six-week-old infant. After resting up and restocking with formula from our friends, we visited as many National Parks as we could over the next three weeks. Camping in free sites or very inexpensive sites was our goal. Food and fuel on the charge card.

I knew I would work one day soon. Ice supplied by Holiday Inns along the way. I made a promise, free ice now and we would be loyal guests in the future. We kept that promise and are Gold Key Members to this day. Consider the promise made, kept.

Once home with my license in hand I began work as a Dentist. Two days a week for Dr. Peter Costa in Villanova, two days a week for Dr. Ashley Botnick in Philadelphia and one evening a week for Dr. Jerry Blum in Philadelphia. I remained dear friends with both Drs. Blum and Botnick until their passing. After a few years of freelancing I decided to start my own practice in Montgomery County, Spring House, Pennsylvania. I designed and built an open office design in an old residential building known as the Denslow House, built in 1939. It was charming and the patients loved it. The practice grew rapidly. By the early 1980s three dental chairs were no longer enough. A new building was going up across the pike. I would design and build an ultra modern, state-of-the-art, dental space and outfit it with the best equipment. Just like that we went from 1939 to 1985 modern. The practice continued to grow and more staff was needed.

I avidly continued my dental education after dental school. I took a two-year program offered by the University of Pennsylvania Dental School in Restorative Dentistry offered by experts in their field. I then began studying with Drs. Ronald Nevins and Howard Skerlow from Boston in Perio Prosthesis. I was awarded a Fellow of the Academy of General Dentistry (FAGD) from the Academy of General Dentistry. Next up was a Master of the Academy of General Dentistry (MAGD), although I was close, retirement was closer. Suffice to say I was strongly committed to my continuing education and that of my staff.

> Proudly we were one of the first dental offices to computerize and to have chair side laptops

Proudly we were one of the first dental offices to computerize and to have chair side laptops for computer generated digital radiographs, which greatly reduces radiographic exposure, as well as providing an almost instant radiograph.

When we decided to move to New Mexico I applied for and, after passing the exams, received my New Mexico Dental license. What was not certain was the outcome of my hand surgery, which in fact it did not go well. Once again, man plans and God laughs. Time to reinvent myself again.

Lessons Learned:

1. The first ten seconds when meeting people are the most important
2. Truly see people and have them feel being seen
3. WOW—Exceed their expectations
4. Under promise and over perform
5. Stand by your work, first and foremost
6. Treat all staff with respect, as all staff is watching

8

1977
2003

ONE DOOR, TWO HOUSES, AND THE LONG WAY HOME

Another trip out west to Taos in 1977, for a winter ski vacation. Just what the Philadelphia winter blues called for. Fresh powder and abundant blue skies day. "Blue Bird" days they call them. We stayed in Taos Ski Valley at Elizabeth and John Bronell's Thunderbird Lodge, a Saturday check in to Saturday check out week.

After a sunny check in, it started to snow the next day; it was pounding. There were large picture windows in the dining room and as the snow continued to fall each day the view out of the window became obscured foot by foot. By the following Saturday there was no view at all! The cars that spent a week in the parking lot were literally buried. A huge front end loader would attach a heavy chain to each car and pull as, one by one, vacationers hoped to leave.. The front end loader gave a pull and the car literally popped out and into the cleared center lane, ready to drive off, hopefully with a good battery for starting. Cars coming up hill for some terrific Saturday powder, usually had one driver and three pushers—quite a sight.

The day before we left I was talking with Elizabeth, the innkeeper, very trim and European with short brown hair. I asked, "When might I pay my bill?" She replied, "Anytime." "Terrific, I will give you my Visa card." She replied, "We only take cash or check." Oops, I had neither. "It is OK, you can send me a check when you get home," she said. Such good people, in such short supply today.

After three days of skiing our legs needed a break, so we ventured down to the town of Taos for some gallery "gazing." One Gallery off of Kit Carson Road was showing furniture by Donald Gardner, a local craftsman, tall and rugged, with wavy long hair. As a furniture maker, I was self sufficient in that department. We had a starter home in the Philadelphia suburbs, and we were looking for land to do our own thing, housewise. As we made our way around the gallery we came upon a door. Not your everyday Home Depot door, but a handmade, unique, "artsy" door. It was replete with funky plugs and playful joinery, copper astrological cut outs fastened to weathered cedar planks. The door had a small one way mirror you could peek out and see who was at your home. Both a serious work of craftsmanship and yet whimsically crafted. Yes, we wanted this piece of the West back East for our future home. We would design the home around the door. It would be both unusual and special, just like the interior swing mini door with the one way mirror on the inside. We had $50 and forked it over, all giddy with excitement. We told Donald that as we could we would mail him a check. Five months later he was paid in full, including shipping. Now we waited, where was the door, we wondered quietly?

My inner fellow said, "Patience my dear Jeff." Before long there was a crate delivered to our driveway. We immediately tore into it with hammer and crowbar. Yes, it was our front door, all the way from Taos. We set the door leaning on our dining room wall, with no other dining room furniture in the room. The door looked nice as wall art. I now settled into designing our future home, inspired by the door. By the Spring of 1979 our new home was going up and the door was being hinged. When the house was completed and we began to entertain, almost everyone who passed through it noticed and commented about how special it was. Phyllis would take pictures of Brett and Rachael on the first day of school each year. Rachael would strike a pose by the door each year.

The years rolled by as they usually do. before long the kids were out of high school and then college. They both decided to move out West to the Rockies. Brett to Taos and Rachael to Denver. Their thinking, if they go we will follow and we did. By the two thousands we were giving serious thought to making our move west a reality. Phyllis had a battle with cancer and that motivated her to act sooner than later. I had my own health challenge, the lunate bone in my right wrist had weakened and twisted due to arthritis. It now sat vertically in the joint, whereas it should be horizontal. The bottom line, the wrist was unstable and limited in motion. Surgical correction was a long shot, and the surgery did in fact fail. Although I did have my New Mexico dental license, my wrist was unstable and with limited motion; dental practice was not possible. Having your career end suddenly with an injury is surreal and unsettling. I felt lost. I had been a dentist for thirty one years. That was my work; it gave me my ability to earn a living and provide for my family. When that rug gets pulled out from under your feet, you feel lost and essentially you are. Finding my way meant redefining myself. Fortunately, woodworking was a possibility if only I could get my right hand to settle down and if not as flexible, but at least more stable.

During the period when we faced all these medical issues, we bought land outside of the town of Taos and began to design what would be our current home. We decided to bring our original "Taos door," 1977, with us. This would entail removing the door from our Pennsylvania home, crating it, and shipping it back to Taos. We would have to buy a Home Depot door and have it installed at the house we were leaving. An expensive but meaningful endeavor to say the least. So the Taos door once again took the long way home back to Taos. The door was installed, the side windows framed in pine were distressed and treated with ammonia and steel wool to give a warm brown patina that I cooked up. Melted paraffin was then brushed over the treated surfaces to give it a timeless look. It was an ironic surprise when our kids first visited and we told them that we would make them keys for the door. OK, they said, but we still have our keys from Pennsylvania. Yes, an ironic coincidence for a door that traveled through now close to fifty years, four thousand miles, two states and two homes, and still found its way home to Taos. Our Granddaughter Olivia has struck the same pose at approximately the same age as her mother, by the very same door, making for a very favorite picture.

Truly a door that invites one in.

I have since built a garden gate for our patio that mirrors the door designs, as well as a requested coffee table for our son's home, that conveys the same magic.

Truly a door that invites one in.

9

A HOME DEFINED
The Hope of Solar and Science

We are shaped by the world around us, and the world of the late seventies was chaotic.

In 1975, shortly after our second child Rachael was born, I opened the doors to my dental practice in Spring House, Pennsylvania. After living in a tract home, I began to design our first home incorporating ideas of solar and energy efficiency. The original Arab oil embargo began in 1973 and seeped into 1974. OPEC imposed its embargo against the United States in retaliation for the US decision to resupply the Israeli military after its war with Egypt. A shortage of oil and gasoline ensued, and long lines of cars were commonplace at gas stations. Eventually tensions eased and the oil flowed. Nothing like the mix of pain and profit.

Fast forward to 1979. Events and political realities in Iran once again triggered an oil crisis of longer gas lines. Iran had ceased exports completely.

During our visits to the Southwest and to New Mexico, which enjoys some three hundred days of sunshine a year, I observed and took notice of homes and historical sites, Canyon de Chelly, Mesa Verde, Chaco Canyon, where they all were oriented to the southern sun. I studied and embraced passive solar design principles.

By 1979 President Jimmy Carter was putting solar panels on the roof of the White House for Solar hot water production. Most important

37

to note, these panels were not to save the planet from climate change, they were to free us from OPEC's use of oil as a tool to blackmail and cause energy pain to the United States. The United States' oil production was through wells that produced much less than what is produced today through fracking and shale mining.

Passive and active solar became necessary design elements in my efforts and my mindset. We bought land that could have a true southern exposure, therefore most windows faced to the south, few to the north, which was mostly hallways and bathrooms. A new design element, skylights would be useful for the north side of the house for ambient lighting. Good windows and thermal shades as well as well-insulated walls rounded out the passive elements. Eleven roof thermal panels would heat the hot water, hot tub, and basement radiator. An airtight wood stove would be the kicker when the sun did

not shine, which in Pennsylvania was sixty percent of the time. Shortly after the completion of our solar home, the Philadelphia Inquirer Sunday Magazine published a piece about the house under the headline, "From Molar to Solar." We enjoyed the piece and had our fifteen minutes of fame. To the best of my knowledge this was the first solar home in Pennsylvania.

The years rolled by, we were using the wood stove almost daily. In the dead of winter, even when the sun shone the days were short. The other unintended consequence of East Coast solar, the mechanics started to break down. The repair costs were exceeding the savings. Our desire to save the earth hit reality.

Thirty years later in the early two thousands we began to design our new home in the Land of Sunshine/ Enchantment, New Mexico. We would surely do passive solar but active would be held off due to our previous Pennsylvania experience with repairs.

We would be passive solar, boiler, and radiant floors with a Kiva fireplace and propane stove for the dining room. All seemed good until it wasn't. Now what came into focus was not the OPEC oil blackmail but global climate change. I dove into the research, Dr. James Hansen's

stood out. For over thirty years he was the director at the Goddard Institute for Space Studies. In 2009 he published his first book, *Storms of my Grandchildren: The Truth about the Coming Climate Catastrophe and our Last Chance to Save Humanity.* The best book on the subject by far. His science seemed sound and surprisingly close twenty years later, in my opinion, understated, inasmuch as we are already close to two degrees Celsius increase in temperature. What was predicted for 2050 is happening now in terms of severe climate change effects.

Our house was designed with a terrific infrastructure, which enabled active solar upgrades. First, thermal solar which tied in directly to our radiant plumbed floors. Six south facing panels catch the heat of the sun which heats the antifreeze circulating back to the house where a heat exchanger transfers the heat to the circulating water back into the coils of the radiant floors. As long as there is electricity for the pumps all is good. A back up if there is no electricity, a wood burning airtight stove will heat the house. Should we not be home, the dining room propane stove thermostat is set for fifty-five degrees to prevent freezing pipes and equipment. Extreme cold or cloudy days would trip the propane boiler to provide heat if needed. All this sequencing is controlled by system specific thermostats.

A few years later we added a photovoltaic array for electricity production. Conveniently we use what we can and the surplus electricity, expressed as kilowatt hours, goes through a reverse meter back into the Kit Carson community grid. Many a month in the spring and fall our electric bill will be between $35 and $45, reflecting the savings produced by the excess kilowatt hours collected by the panels. This is our way of helping our grandchildren and the planet.

For further flexibility and comfort in winter heating and summer cooling we installed three strategically placed reverse cycle heat pumps. Our Kit Carson electric provider is one hundred percent solar and with battery storage capabilities. Therefore and fortunately our kilowatt hour cost is quite reasonable, which makes the reverse cycle heat pumps very efficient. We increased our comfort and reduced our carbon footprint as well. I believe that climate goals have been surpassed negatively, therefore it is time for mitigation strategies. Can science save our planet? There is a chance, there is hope.

There is a chance,
there is hope.

10   1982 1983

THE TRIATHLON
Two Birds, One Stone

By 1981, I had some modest athletic achievements. I could swim a mile, bike ride a hundred miles (a "century"), and I had climbed Mount Washington in the winter on ice and snow. But I still did not feel accomplished athletically.

Although I played ice and roller hockey, baseball, football, and a bit of golf, I was quite unaccomplished, a so-so athlete. In 1981, the movie "Chariots of Fire" was released. Based on the true story of two British athletes training and competing in the 1924 Olympics, an historical sports drama. The musical theme, both beautiful and inspirational, was written by Vangelis. In fact, it won the Academy Award for best original score.

So I am sitting in the theater and I find myself getting motivated and excited to do something athletically inspiring. I vaguely recalled reading about this new event in Hawaii called a Triathlon. It began in 1978, as a swim, bike, run event. The movie kept on rolling, as my mind and heart were already racing. As the movie ended my dream began. I would train for and compete in the most challenging Triathlon that I could.

I had all the equipment needed except for a pair of New Balance Running shoes! I ordered four magazines; *Triathlon, Running, Biking* and *Swim* magazines, as well as Dr. Gabe Merkin's *The Sports Medicine Book*, a veritable bible for sports injuries and recoveries.

In addition to training for the three major events, there was strength/weight training and stretching that needed to be done. I would run before work in the morning, swim during my lunch break in the afternoon, and alternate weight training and biking after work. Stretching was done with professionals in Philadelphia twice a week in the evenings.

I signed up for the Philadelphia Masters Triathlon. to be held in Philadelphia and Atlantic City in June of 1982. Training in the Philadelphia suburbs in the winter is no easy task. The weather is not conducive to outdoor running or biking. Spring came around and the final countdown began, along with extensive outdoor workouts.

The Philadelphia Masters was a sanctioned Masters event and competition was by age grouping. The swim started in the Bay outside of Harrah's Casino and Hotel in Atlantic City and rounded up in the Atlantic Ocean. Jumping in, even though it was a sunny day, the water felt cold at first but a few hundred yards into the one mile swim and all I could feel was the experience, stroke after stroke, rhythmic breathing, the lifting arc of my arms to keep out of the chop, using my head to create an air space for breathing air and not water. Open water swimming in a triathlon has another challenge, which way

to go and how to go there straight and direct. Every fifth stroke you push down with your right hand enough to lift your head and chest upward, whereupon you can get a quick view of the buoy or marker you are heading towards. It is not easy, but it sure beats going off course or tacking a zig zag course. It was comforting to know the life guards seemed to be following everyone, everywhere, from the safety and comfort of their life boats. Through open water and with chop like waves it was hard to find markers. This was not an easy swim. Gratefully sharks and jelly fish were not on the program that day. Even more gratefully the race came to an end with a ladder climb out of the inner harbor to a pier, which most gratefully had a line of outdoor rinse off showers set up. One could only imagine what I just swam through. Certainly not your local pool, all filtered and chlorinated. Day one completed and on Saturday the bike race.

The bike race was one rider at a time and against the clock, a sprint from the steps (think Rocky) of the Philadelphia Art Museum to the East River Drive, over the Strawberry Mansion Bridge, back down the West River Drive to the finish line. I clocked in at 22.5 miles/hour, good enough to finish in third place. My highest finish in any discipline at any event, in any sport, ever.

Sunday's run was not my favorite event and probably explains why I have so little memory of it.

All in all, a good taste of what a triathlon was about. Even though spread over three days, instead of the usual three events in one day, one after another and at much greater distances and more extreme weather.

More intense training and mental toughness would have to be honed and sharpened for the 1983 Anthracite Triathlon, held in Jim Thorpe, Pennsylvania. The Olympic distance event included a one mile open water swim in Mauch Chunk Lake, a thirty mile bike ride, and a ten-mile run, ending in the heart of town on Main Street.

The race started on a very warm morning in July. My advice in a group swimming race—if you are on the slow side, enter the water toward the back of the pack. Enter early and you will have to contend with a lot of chop and with other swimmers swimming literally over you.

After the swim the late morning sun felt nice and warming, but it was time to get my bike shirt, shorts, and shoes on. Hop on the bike and the first thing that hits you is that you are no longer swimming, all different body mechanics and balance taking place. The trick is to find your rhythm before you find the pavement. With thirty miles to go on the bike and ten miles of running, pacing yourself, energy management and time sequencing all start to come into play. Go too fast and you will crash or hit the proverbial wall on the run. Pace yourself, nourish, and hydrate just so. Time sequencing matters little in a one hundred yard dash, but it matters an awful lot in a long race. Break it down from thirty miles on the bike to one mile, one minute at a time, your goal is not the whole of it, just small intervals of time and distance. You are starting to get tired but you do not have to deal with the entirety of the bike distance plus the run, in the moment. Just one mile, one minute at a time—small manageable physical and mental goals.

CARBON COUNTY TRIATHLON
JULY 17, 1983

As the bike race ended I realized how hot and humid it had gotten. I still had a ten mile run to do. The transition from bike to running was even more dramatic and challenging. The legs were cycling but the event was running. Once again the required rhythm evolved. By early afternoon, the sun was beating down on me, I was no longer on the cool waters of the morning swim. There was no longer the welcome breeze on the bike. The ten mile run was not only the last event but also presented the challenge of lasting. As a matter of course, the first six or seven miles of running will come easily. I soon became aware of a caravan of ambulances behind the pack. The heat index was dangerously high and as the temperatures rose the runners fell. Paramedics would scoop them up and IV them in the ambulance. Step by step, a stride of five feet would be made. More and more it was clear that just to finish would be a victory in and of itself. Five feet down, five feet less to go, a good mind game to play. Another conscious thought, you could hit the "wall" at any moment, you could be stricken with dehydration, heat stroke, or muscle cramping. Danger was lurking, the notion of terminating from this triathlon and so close to the finish line was all too real. The group I was in rounded a corner and we found ourselves on Main Street, not far from the finish line. The ominous caravan of ambulances was still behind us. As I rounded that corner a pleasant surprise was before me. Both sides of Main Street were lined by houses. The towns people lined the street and with their hoses

> ... to finish would be a victory in and of itself.

turned on transformed a brutally hot July day into a cooling and most welcoming "rain" shower. Relief and rejuvenation, a reminder of a town with thoughtful and compassionate folks, I am forever grateful. A few moments later with the "rain" shower and trees behind us we were out in the open, exposed to the sun but with only few hundred yards to go. Just before I crossed the finish line I passed below the local banks thermometer, reading ninety-nine degrees. In moments my Triathlon was done. My next recollection was going to a local cafe and literally ordering the left side of the menu. The pierogies were especially delicious. I did not win nor place in the race, but I did win the raffle drawing, a family white water trip down the Monongahela River. A trip we enjoyed as a family.

It is obvious that physical strength and cardiovascular fitness is a needed benefit of training and racing. Less obvious is your ability to manage the challenge of this endurance race through emotional management. Even more subtle is the notion that if I can handle this I can have the resolve and resilience to deal with much that life can dish out: "I have the physical and emotional reserves." What started as a "Chariot of Fire" to prove outer physical strength and performance resulted in the discovery of inner strength and resilience. Two birds one stone.

Photo by Jeffrey Hills

11 1986

LAKE POWELL AND HAVASU FALLS
The Blue Green Water and the Four Horses of Havasu

In 1972, Phyllis and I were riding along on highway 89 in northern Arizona in our Toyota FJ40 Landcruiser, yesteryear's version of today's SUV. It was one hundred degrees plus, and there was no air conditioning. Our infant son Brett was in the back, actually in a hammock slung across the "B" pillars behind the driver and passenger seats. To dampen the up and down pitching a bungee was wrapped around the netting and affixed to the floor. It was so hot that the pavement was shimmering. You could see the heat roiling up in layers. The print map laid out our route into Utah pretty clearly. But looking out in the distance something looked strange. As we drew closer the clear shimmering turned blue. This was mysterious, especially in the high desert of northern Arizona. The closer we got the blue back ground seemed to go forever. Actually it was a body of water and it was not marked on our gas station fold-up paper map.

A detour was in order. The main road led us to an access road, the sign read, Lake Powell Reservoir, United States Corps of Army Engineers. Water is water and most welcoming, we drove right onto the beach. We put two branches in the ground and laid a large towel over a cardboard box where our son lay, protected from the sun. Phyllis and I ran straight into the cooling blue water. We were actually in the Wahweap area and we were the only ones in sight. What a refreshing delight.

Beyond the delight of the moment, a fifty-plus year connection with our family and Lake Powell began.

In 1986, when our kids were in school we went to Lake Powell for our family summer vacations. We completed the rental and orientation of our 36' house boat and off we cruised. Our final destination, where we would stay for several days was Good Hope Bay. I sat and stared at the shoreline and the conformity of the shapes. The flat tops of the mesas and buttes, their profiles shifting from vertical to angled to vertical to angled again and again.

I began to draw on my tablet, soon becoming aware of not only this simple but naturally aesthetic formation but how it could transition to a furniture design. This "mesa" design formed the conceptual basis of the three dining room cabinets I built in the 1980s. All three cabinets were published in Fine Woodworking Magazine and are still with us today. They form our heirloom legacy furniture, tied to our history and memories.

After our trip, which was relaxing and pleasurable for the family, it was time for something more adventuresome.

We left Wahweap early in the morning and drove hours to the Havasu Falls trailhead. The plan: park, gear up, hike down to the primitive motel, set up camping gear to prepare our freeze dried dinner. With backpacks strapped on we began the eight-mile trip down the steep switch backs. It did not take long before we all realized how long the trip would be. The weight of the packs, the soft sand. This was not the same as an afternoon stroll through the mall. Rachael, our youngest had it the toughest. Brett volunteered to carry her pack after she threw it on the ground and started to cry. All of this trail and the canyon which carried the Havasu River over three falls, Havasu, Navajo ,and Mooney are all integral to the river and they all feed the Grand Canyon's Colorado River.

The waters are all a bright blue-green due to a high concentration of the minerals, calcium carbonate and magnesium. This also accounts for the travertine deposits, which add even more beauty to this magically beautiful and wondrous place.

All of this land is the Tribal land of the Havasupai Tribe.

All of this land is the Tribal land of the Havasupai Tribe. To this day they still abide by the ancient traditions and prayers. You are guests on their land and they make you very aware of that by their watchful presence.

Most meals we prepared were on the picnic tables out front of the motel. It was an easy two mile hike to Havasu Falls. The hike was comfortable with a firm trail and large trees to provide shady protection from the sun. Havasu falls and the pool beneath were magically beautiful. The water was seventy degrees or so, just right for the heat of the day. There was a large gnarly tree with an ample horizontal branch to which a thick rope that hung from it was just right for a swing over the water followed by "letting go" and enjoying a cool splash into the water, all of which the kids enjoyed and Phyllis as well.

The days went by quickly and before long it was time for the return trip, which was all uphill, and eight miles back to the car. We had arranged for four saddle horses and the Havsupai wranglers had a few mules, tied to their horses, to carry our packs and the outgoing mail. It did not take long before this friendly group of horses and mules began to play this game of kick the animal behind you. Problem was, one of us was always on the animal behind. At one point we lost Rachael, her horse took a detour to go back home for a break. Altogether again, we continued to endure the kicking and biting that would break out from time to time. I think our wranglers were entertained by this and it was not the first time either.

Finally, arriving in the packed dirt parking lot, we were happy to be off horseback in one piece, gathered our gear, loaded the car and began the first leg of the long trip home to Philadelphia. I am sure we have four different versions of the experience and I am sure they are all good.

. . . a more innocent time . . .

12 1984

IN DAYS GONE BY
The Way We Were

What was life like in the mid-1980s? I am no historian but perhaps this short story will describe a more innocent time in our country and the world.

I was on a solo camping and hiking trip in Moab, Utah, in Canyonlands National Park. A wonderful long October weekend, 4X4 jeeping, hiking, and sleeping under a rock outcropping in the Needles district enjoying the cool air and the super cool nocturnal sky. After my camping and hiking was done, I spent Sunday night in the closest town, Monticello. With a large bag of popcorn and a six pack, I was set for dinner. Early the next morning I headed over to the very small Moab Regional Airport. There were two other guys so that made three of us who were looking for our pilot who was nowhere to be found. He was to fly us to Salt Lake City Airport. One of the guys found the pilot's home phone number (this is before cell phones). He called him, and in fact woke him up. He was soon ready to leave his house, but given the departure time of my flight back to Philadelphia, it looked tight. The pilot, a young guy with a blond crew cut, finally shows up and barks out, "I need some hands, we have to push the plane over to the fuel tank, we need fuel." OK, I figure so I will miss my flight, probably there will be another.

I sat in the copilot's seat, yoke and all while the two other passengers sat behind us with the baggage stowed in the tail section.

We had to traverse the Wasatch Mountain Range with a peak altitude of 11,928 feet. A single prop plane must find the passes (gaps) and fly through. It was during this critical time in the flight that the pilot confided in me that he was desperate to pee. I could and did give him verbal comfort, but that was as far as I was going. This was a no "pee" flight, after all. I thought as we went through the pass to the Salt Lake City side of the Range that I could tell him my concern, "Mr. Pilot I am going to miss my flight home." He responded, "I will call ahead and notify your airline that you will be late." I am thinking to myself, "Yeah right, like they care."

The pilot made his call and then got his landing instructions from the tower. We made our initial approach to land and a left bank brought us straight in line with the runway. Throttled down, flaps employed, speed reduced, and touch down. At this point General Aviation usually goes to the far side of the airport. Instead the pilot turns in toward the big airline planes at their gates. He tells me that my airline is holding the plane for me and taxis to my gate door on the tarmac. He literally stops our plane fifty feet from the door. I jump out, grab my back pack, made my way up two flights of steps, I come out another door directly onto the gang way, leading to the plane's entry door. The stewardess greets me, grabs and stows my pack in the over head compartment. My pack had a camping stove and fuel, as well as my six inch hunting knife. No sooner am I seated than the plane pushes back, taxis to his runway, throttles up, and takes off, wheels up, homeward bound. No more than ten minutes from my arrival till take off. There was no TSA, or baggage inspections...just trust, decency and fellowship. This is the way we were, in days gone by. Trust and decency lost is so hard to rebuild, but I still hold hope for my grandkids.

13 1994

FRANCE
First Destination: Normandy

So many weddings, so many times I sat with Uncle David, Phyllis' Aunt Irene's husband. As an executive of El-Al Airlines he was comped air fare to anywhere in the world. His favorite—the French country side. I would spend the wedding hearing the fine details of a Normandy goat cheese. His formula was straight forward. Go to one village, rent a cottage, stay for a month and then go out and explore. In his case essentially, sample all the wine and cheese the region had to offer.

A French guide book's appendix listed travel advisors they recommended. We decided on Henri Scharff, French born and now working in New York City as a boutique travel agent. He laid out a plan for us and delightfully it worked out wonderfully and in fact exceeded our expectations.

On the eve of the fiftieth anniversary of D-Day we flew to Paris over night. Sitting in a coach seat, nearly upright, was not conducive to a restful night. We arrived tired but excited the next morning. We gathered our bags and went to pick up our rental car, only to find a special available, a 190E Mercedes Benz five speed. We took the special and shortly rode off into the country side to visit the Monet estate in Giverny. We were traveling on a main route when we came upon an expansive toll booth plaza. Confusion swept over me, was there Easy Pass? Exact money lanes? Pay a toll keeper? All signs were in French and I was sure they would want French money and not American dollars! This was day one, hour two and on three hours of sleep.

53

Time for a pause, I pulled to the far right and studied the lanes. Finally I figured out the most likely to have a toll collector, the slowest one. I pulled the car in and handed over a twenty-franc note. The toll officer eyed me with annoyance and gave me $19.50 change.

We enjoyed a stroll through Monet's gardens, loving the delicate wooden bridges arched over the narrows of the ponds. Before long we were back in the car on the highway heading further into the country side.

Henri had us booked at a farm in the Normandy country side. Our accommodations were a small suite above the barn. We arrived late in the afternoon and were greeted by the host, a lovely French woman with gray brown hair. Our second challenge, she did not speak English and on day one our French did not go much beyond the pleasantries of the day. The gist of our question was "When will dinner be served?" We were told with a combination of French, English and hand gestures, "There would not be dinner, but we could go to town for our meal." I explained that we have come over night from Philadelphia, with little sleep and could not drive. She understood and assured us, no worries and went back to the main house. She returned a short time later with a platter of cheese, French bread, grapes, and a bottle of red wine complete with two glasses. She sat us at a table in the garden, with a view of the setting sun. Uncle David would be proud. We ate, we drank, and by eight we slept. The next morning, with bodies nourished and rested we explored the towns and beaches of Normandy. The culture and the history, especially that of June 6, 1944, the allied D-Day invasion to free Europe, foremost in our mind. We were fascinated by the small war history museums that dotted the coast, set right into the towns. Nothing more touching though then the Allied Cemeteries, so well manicured, so sad in their row upon row of fallen soldiers, who fought, who fell, and there we stood with heavy hearts and reverence. Boys and men who lived to fight, but never lived to live a life well lived. Before long the sun was setting.

Second Destination: Brittany

Days later we traveled to Brittany, before the Causway was built where the tidal coast makes the Island of Mont-Saint-Michel only accessible every twelve hours during slack and low tide. Surprisingly, it seemed that the only dish available at any restaurant on any menu was moules/mussels. I was not sure Phyllis was going to eat that day but, it turned out that she loved the moules and to this day it has become a special meal for us.

We were staying at a small bed and breakfast in a quaint village well off the coast in farm country. I was ready to swim in the pool I thought they had, only to find out from the proprieter (Jacques) that the pool was in the next town over. (I recalled the guide book stated "Pool nearby.") Sensing my disappointment he offered us two old-school, no shift bicycles for a spin around the country side. What a wonderful experience, simply divine. Farms, cows and French farm houses were all on the visual menu.

Jacques and an assistant served us a delicious French dinner featuring a crispy duck, the sides, the salads and the desserts—all lovely.

Jacques then took the dinner group into a sitting room off the dining area. He poured us each a small serving of an after dinner drink that was not familiar. The brandy glass was filled with ethereal vapors that literally knocked your head back and made your eyes water. This was not your every day digestif!

Jacques finished his pouring and we continued our careful sipping while he shared a story. We were drinking twenty-five year old Calvados du Pays D'Auge that is made from apples and aged for twenty-five years, resulting in a very high percent of alcohol by volume. Jacques then moved to the wall where photographs in black and white hung. Most were of World War II. He explained that the Allies needed food and he needed fuel for his tractors. A deal was made—food for fuel. After the war he began bottling his, to-be, twenty-five year old Calvados. As we were leaving in the morning I asked about it. He went to a cabinet and brought me a fresh bottle beautifully labeled and sealed, old world style with red wax. For many years afterwards, dinner with family and friends would end with a very small serving in a brandy glass. This went on for about ten years, then I ran out. My son was on a trip to France and brought a bottle home to me. Although it was the same, maybe the difference was Jacques.

Driving around the French country side had an unexpected culinary surprise. Around midday, when driving through a French village you would look for someone walking or riding a bike. Inevitably there would be a baguette laying in a bicycle basket or under an arm. You would see from whence they came and head in that direction. Soon finding the bakery, enter and say to the help "Une baguette machete s'il vous plait" (one baguette, cut in half if you please). Add to that some cheese, a day wine, and ham, find a tree to park under, and call it a gourmet French lunch.

With five more days to explore the usual tourist highlights of Paris, a wonderful European experience indeed.

14   2000 2002

ONE BOAT, TWO ADVENTURES
The Sea Calls for Seamanship

After our house boat on Lake Powell ran its course of enjoyment, we looked closer to home for the more challenging tidal waters of the Chesapeake Bay. We took the Coast Guard Marine Safety Course as well as a hands-on course for certification in Fort Myers, Florida. I read the nautical bible, Chapman's, cover to cover. We were set. Our first boat on the Chesapeake was a 32-foot Island Gypsy trawler. A well founded, full displacement vessel with wooden decks, topsides, and below decks as well. She was a good boat, but had a cruising speed of only six knots WOT (wide open throttle) and not much more. This lack of speed was a disadvantage during the sudden thunder storms that came up during the summer. The speed or lack thereof also limited what you could do in a weekend, Friday through Sunday.

After seven years on Ramblin Rose, the Island Gypsy Trawler, we went to the Annapolis Boat Show in Maryland. While there we met Steve Zimmerman, a boat builder extraordinaire (and in his spare time a martial arts teacher), well spoken, of the highest ethics and integrity. We saw his beautiful Z-36 Down East Cruiser. I slept with the brochure on my night table for a year, and then we decided to go to Virginia to have a visit and find out more about this beautiful cruising boat.

Designs, electronics, safety issues were discussed and put into the mix for an initial quote. We agreed that I would build the interior saloon table and entertainment cabinet.

The electronics and safety gear were all designed with redundancy (backup) in mind. For example, one main VHF radio with its own dedicated antennae. Then a less expensive but serviceable radio with its own dedicated antennae. If on deck or in the unsinkable dinghy, a water proof portable hand held with a belt clip would be needed. Today, a water proof cell phone would round out emergency communications. Of course we would have an EPIRB on board, which automatically identifies our position and vessel name, and sends an SOS signal out to satellites. Today, the best equipped boats would have smaller EPIRBS that are affixed to each life vest, as well.

The hull would be built in Maine, a Down East, Spencer Lincoln design. Known for use in lobster boats off the Maine coast. Just right for cutting through the short chop of the Chesapeake Bay. The boat would be powered by a single screw Cummins 300 hp turbo diesel. She would cruise at 14–15 knots and at WOT(Wide Open Throttle) 17–18 knots. The boat had a semi-planing hull, and she cut a fine line through the water. The short chop and waves of the Bay were all manageable. All the arrangements were made and Rosewood would be launched in the spring of 2000.

Rosewood

Both our grandmother's were named "Rose" and wood was my pleasure and passion. Rosewood was my most highly prized species to work with. I built our dining room furniture in Rosewood.

In the spring we took possession of Rosewood and began the best cruising years of our maritime lives. For extended cruising we had two spare fuel tanks and a large triangular auxiliary water tank up forward toward the bow. The galley sported an auxiliary freezer/refrigerator for extra storage of perishables, in addition to the standard nautical refrigerator/freezer combo. There is always a weak link—ours was trash storage; just plan on it.

Our first major trip was the Chesapeake Bay to Port Jefferson, Long Island, off the Long Island Sound. On our departure date we set out at first light going north on the Chesapeake to the C and D Canal, heading northeast for fourteen miles to the mouth of the Delaware River and Delaware Bay. Our timing and day plan was going well. We took an east compass setting and set the GPS chart map for Cape May. The tide was running out but the wind picked up and was running inshore against the tide. This was not good, but we had a Spencer Lincoln hull and she was built for this. The Delaware Bay's 5-8-feet waves with a short chop were quite the challenge. The period or time between wave crests was becoming a challenge as well. Crests were upon us so rapidly that we had little time to course correct or recover. Forget lunch, hold our bearings steady, and hit our way points to Cape May. Fourteen knots made good and we would have an ETA in four hours. Phyllis, navigating the GPS and chart plotter all did well. With a steady hand on the wheel, we were tied up in time for dinner and a stiff drink.

We left Cape May early and headed out of the Cape May Inlet to reach the Atlantic Ocean. The Inlet at first was a bit choppy and then began to roll with the lengthened period of the ocean (time between waves), I grew a bit queasy, but as we picked up speed I settled down. As we came out of the Inlet, we turned to port to head North to New York City and stayed parallel to the Jersey Shore, using radar rings for course guidance to stay two miles off shore.

By afternoon we began to enter Lower Hudson Bay and could on this clear day see the World Trade Towers, so tall and proud with sparkled sun reflection. This was the summer of 2000, a little over a year before they tragically came down on September 11, 2001. Neither I nor anyone else would see the Lower Manhattan skyline the same, nor have the same world view. We left Lower Manhattan to our port and entered the East River. Passing under all the famous bridges was exciting, especially the Brooklyn Bridge with it views of Manhattan. We were no longer cruising on open waters. The traffic on the water was intense. The rules of, right-of-way were essential. Another challenge was coming. Where the Long Island Sound meets the East River is known as "Hells Gate." There are significant tidal currents, swirling waters with holes in them, and standing waves of up to eight feet. This presented challenging boating issues, both navigation and piloting. The goal is to hit the "gate" at slack tide or thereabouts. Second choice, have the tide and current with you, with little to no opposing wind. Third choice, be sure your insurance is paid up to date.

Here is a small section of water so dangerous that if at all possible build or buy your boat to deal with it. Planning properly is best, powering through should at least be a choice. We made it both ways on a combination of planning and power.

We tied up at Port Jefferson Marina and for three days entertained friends and family who came to visit us on our new boat. Life was grand.

Life was grand.

Another year, another vacation. This time south to Norfolk Beach, Virginia, which sounds relaxing and it is. The cruise started in the upper Chesapeake Bay at our marina on Lankford Creek. To leave the Chesapeake Bay and reach the Atlantic Ocean you will take the main shipping channel, which joins the Thimble Shoal Channel, for our final leg. All this is happening on the water between two artificial islands protected by high granite rocks. These two islands form the entrance and exit to the Chesapeake Bay Bridge Tunnel.

A nice five days on the beach and a visit to a Navy destroyer open to the public. While on the destroyer an officer told me that he anticipated heavy weather coming into the naval base and was planning a "sortie," which means a dispatch from a strong point, which is to say, a Naval vessel is safer moving in the water than it is tied up to its berth and potentially subject to structural damage.

The forecast for the day we were to leave called for rising seas and wind, but no small craft warnings. A small craft warning is a Coast Guard guide line and considering our vessel and her sea worthiness, we could push that envelope a bit.

As we left our dock it was sunny, windy, and dark clouds were moving in. A truism; there are some situations where high stakes are a possibility and there are some situations where you will be in the thick of it and dealing with it. We were about to experience the difference, and at the higher end of the spectrum.

The seas were building, I asked Phyllis for some coffee. She replied, "No can do!" The trouble had started, the adventure had begun. The radio channel, WX1, marine forecast for offshore Virginia Beach had been updated and upgraded to, "four to six foot seas with small craft warnings." We were about thirty percent into the toughest part of our trip, returning to the Bay. First there were the steep waves of the Atlantic to

The trouble had started, the adventure had begun.

deal with. Then on to the Thimble Shoal Channel between the two artificial islands, protected by islands of granite boulders. On entering the Chesapeake the waves would be confused, coming from multiple directions, as often happens when two different bodies of water meet.

The wind plus wave direction was such that I could not steer the course heading into the channel. For safety sake I had to tack a course in a zigzag fashion, always trying to go into the waves at a forty-five degree or so angle. We were on a course to take us into the channel and proceed to tack our heading accordingly. Going through a channel with two rocky islands on both sides would be difficult if there was boat traffic. On a day like today, there wouldn't be much traffic—or would there be? In our path heading toward us was a United States Naval Destroyer, all six hundred and ten feet of her with a sixty-foot beam. The right of way belonged to the Naval vessel, "The rule of gross tonnage," and she had guns!

We were forced into another challenge. Take evasive action and deal with the ocean conditions. I had to change my tack ninety degrees to starboard, from the port approach I was on. The VHF radio was set for dual signal, channel sixteen for hailing the Coast Guard and channel thirteen for bridge to bridge and I would guess US Naval Destroyers as well. At six hundred feet the destroyer seemed quite steady in the water. At forty-two feet LOA we were taking a beating. This is what they called snotty conditions and we were taking on green sea water over the bow. At times I felt like we were a submarine. We were not able to get the bow over the largest waves, so the power would push it through. Fortunately, our multiple strong bilge pumps along with ample scuppers to shed the water astern served us well. The ninety degree turn meant that instead of heading into the channel we were now heading to the rocky island.

My goal was to buy time in order to get that "right of way" destroyer into the channel and out. We had gone from taking seas off the starboard bow quarter to now taking them off the port bow quarter.

As the destroyer began to pass the islands and with the rocks getting closer, my time to make my move had come. Waves usually come in sets with the same period, but every three to five waves there is usually a pause of a few seconds.

I was going to use that pause to my advantage to turn ninety degrees to port and put us on a course away from the rocks and back toward the channel, slipping in astern of the destroyer.

With rocks looming, green water on my windshield, wipers useless, I sensed my moment and turned the wheel hard and fast to port. The boat turned and exposed her starboard hull to the waves and a possible broach. As planned and hoped for the next wave we picked up was on our stern. We rode it out to sea and the channel. One more easier turn into the waves set us on a course through the channel and into the Bay. Conditions were a bit better and considering there were no destroyers or rocks, perhaps a whole lot better.

We were feeling a bit whipped and the thought of tying up and having an adult beverage was sounding rather attractive. We turned up into the Elizabeth River, and found a marina for the night. We were berthed next to a beautiful forty-two foot Hinckley Down East cruiser, built in Maine. The captain asked me how it was out there? I told him and he respectfully scoffed and said he would give it a go. An hour or so later, just as I was wondering how he was doing, he returned. He told me it was pretty tough out there. We were, after all, two Maine Down East cruisers on the same page.

15 2003

CROSSING PATHS AGAIN
Edward Abbey, Naturalist, Conservationist

The decades rolled by, so quickly at times feeling like a freight train speeding nonstop across the rails at a crossing.

While exploring the feasibility of a mid-fifties move to New Mexico, I discovered *Just Enough,* a book written by Harvard Business Schools professors Dr. Laura Nash and Dr. Howard Stevenson. The key interview for the book takes place at Valley of the Gods Bed and Breakfast, a five star inn near Goosenecks State Park off the nearby San Juan River, that is to say, an isolated B and B in the middle of the southern Utah desert. Its thick stone walls are off the electrical grid. Photovoltaic solar and a gas generator provide all the power needed.

In 2005 we rode our motorcycle from Taos, New Mexico, to Mexican Hat, Utah, for our first stop on our trip. The road to the Bed and Breakfast was quite rough and very dusty, but we did find our way.

When passing through Shiprock, New Mexico, we stopped and picked up a steak and some trimmings at a local market. The inn's propane powered refrigerator was up to the task of keeping our food cold and fresh. After checking in, a hot shower surrounded by eighteen

65

inch thick stone walls was refreshing and unique. The wood floors, low wooden ceiling and stone walls spoke of a storied history.

After a hike and wash up it was time to fire up the barbecue and do the steak justice. The wooden deck creaked of a time gone by. Most comforting were the two cottonwood trees surrounding the deck and table offering a welcome shade. They seemed so out of place, however, the only trees around for miles. With my curiosity running high I asked the innkeeper about the tall, shady cottonwoods.

"They were planted in the 1970s by a National Park Superintendent, Edward Abbey," he told me. Every now and then Abbey would return with buckets of water to quench their thirsts. So here we were again, some thirty years since Elephant Hill in Canyonlands and some fifty years since Edward Abbey planted and nurtured the shade trees we were sitting under and where we were enjoying our steak dinner. Once more Abbey added an extra dimension to my enjoyment and appreciation of the West.

The cool stone walls kept the room just right for a good night's rest. A hearty breakfast in the morning and off to Monument Valley for a motorcycle ride through the valley floor of the Navajos.

16

2013
2015
2018

THE MOTOR VESSEL DAVID B
On the Water, Where I Long to Be

Our move from Pennsylvania to Taos in 2003 had many pluses, notably closeness to our children and better opportunities for woodworking. There is always a catch—no water, no boating. Of course we have some reservoirs and lakes. Our first effort to fill this void motivated us to build a sixteen foot sail/row boat. A beautiful wood and epoxy hand built effort. Fun, though that it was, there is nothing quite like the thump thump thump of a diesel engine working while singing its singular notes.

In the Fall of 2012 I hit the internet looking for small boat cruises in Alaska's Inside Passage. Near the top of the list was Northwest Passages, offering spring and fall long weekends in Washington State out of Bellingham, San Juan Islands (technically the Salish Sea) on the David B. During the summer months, eight-day inside passage cruises from Juneau to Ketchikan, Alaska, and back again.

The David B is a 1929 Trawler, powered by a Washington Iron Works three-cylinder diesel, 100 hp engine. It was originally a "tow" boat. It would pick up fishing boats, that could not have engines as per the law, in the morning and leave them in the fishing grounds. Later that afternoon the David B would pick them up and tow them to the fish processing boats to offload their catch, then take them back to their home ports.

67

Although one hundred horse power sounds underpowered, the David B has a full displacement hull, meaning that it does not plane or semi-plane. It essentially cruises at hull speed, which for a 65-foot boat is six to eight knots. The Washington one hundred horse power diesel is more than up to that task. In 1998, just as the David B was to be scrapped, she was rescued by Jeffrey and Christine Smith. They refurbished the boat from stem to stern. Making it ready for its second life as a ship for passenger service.

In late Summer 2015 we decided to try a four-day San Juan Island cruise before we committed to an eight-day Alaska trip.

It was terrific. Our Captain Jeffrey Smith is licensed for one hundred tons, as is his wife Christine. She is also a naturalist and culinary master. Waking up to Christine's Belgium chocolate filled croissants with a carafe of fresh brewed rich coffee—well, if for no other reason, that is why you wake up.

Captain Jeff and I hit it off right away. The pilot house has ample room for guests and lively conversations. He invited me to take the helm of the David B. Fortunately on our plane flight I brushed up on the Coast Guard Rules of the Road. I also familiarized myself with the new AIS (Automatic Identification System). The bottom line, know your course, identify any other vessels' range, direction, and speed. Stay on course. Follow the Rules of the Road and of utmost importance, avoid collisions at all cost. Captain Jeff was confident in my ability and before long would leave me on the bridge while he relaxed nearby.

During a casual conversation Captain Jeff asked me to design and build a custom nautical style and grade medicine cabinet for the forward head and wet room. It was beautifully done in teak and spalted maple with bronze marine hardware. Captain Jeff very generously offered us a discount on our eight-day Alaska trip in 2015.

In Alaska I did two shifts a day on most days at the helm. I enjoyed navigating and steering on course for the David B Because of her weight and length she would hold a true course, as long as you did not oversteer. Course corrections were to be made slowly and incrementally to avoid a zig zag course of inefficiency and futility. I enjoyed and valued Captain Jeff's respect and trust for my boating skills. This was, after all a commercial vessel carrying six to eight passengers. I had a good time and was most grateful for his trust.

While on this Alaska trip we would motor into coves that would lead us to calving glaciers, filling the passage way with icebergs of all sizes. There was a stationary exercise bike on the upper deck. I jumped on and began to pedal away, cold and with a biting wind in my face, with the most magnificent scenery one could imagine. The water was filled with white/blue icebergs, the greenery of the surrounding mountains and straight ahead the incredible beauty of the calving glacier. This is what a "biker's high" is all about.

Whale sightings, especially when the whales were feeding in pods, was thrilling and most camera worthy. What terrific memories and pictures. In one moment, just as I was about to take the wheel, a whale did a full breach not more than twenty feet from me.

Later in the trip Captain Jeff spoke to me about a custom coffee table for their salon, which was to under go a refit that coming winter. The coffee table would be Oak with more "beef" and my usual arched base.

It had to be able to withstand the rigors of a nautical life. The project was a success, as described on the David B website, "We are proud to have a custom coffee table created specifically for the David B, by master woodworker Jeffrey Hills, from the Taos Woodshop."

Captain Jeff and Christine invited us to join them as their guests to the Victoria, Canada, Wooden Boat Show in lieu of payment. Another great cruise and enjoyable experience.

Many memories from our trips on the David B, maybe another trip in the future. Something to think about while my body settles into bed at night, and my mind can almost hear the clapping of the waves slapping at the hull sides as I drift off to a peaceful sleep on the water, where I long to be.

17 2016

A HORSE NAMED CHARLIE
A Dear Friend Named Larry

On January 18, 2016, Taos lost its revered physician, Dr. Larry Schreiber. Phyllis and I lost a dear friend from our school days and through college. His ashes and memorial were held up where he loved to be, in the high country, 11,205 feet to be exact, at a meadow at the end of Gavilan Trail. Although in a beautiful alpine meadow, the trip up the narrow trail is both steep and challenging. The Gavilan Trail out and back is a total of 5.7 miles. The rate of climb is the highest in the area, one thousand feet per mile. Physically in my late sixties and with back issues, I did not feel that I could get up there on my own. While working on a table restoration for my client Lois, a lovely and petite woman, she asked me to deliver her finished table to her storage unit near town.

I met her there and when she opened the door I noticed a saddle. A beauty, with embossed leather features and tassels. I asked her if she rode. Lois told me she was an expert rider. I told her of my desire to get up to the meadow and wishing to do it on horseback. She knew Larry and wanted to help. She sensed my pain and need.

Lois told me that although she had the saddle, she did not have the horse. However, her friend Kimberly did have horses, so off to Kimberly, in Ranchos de Taos. I found the stables and shortly met a personable tall strong woman dressed in full western wear, and yes, that includes the hat.

She told me it was a most difficult trail and that in spite of my riding experience she would give me a crash course while on my horse Charlie. I would also have to wear a helmet. This turned out to be smart advice.

A few weeks later Lois, Kimberly, and I loaded up the trailer with our three steeds for the trip to the trailhead, which is off the ski road.

The horses were saddled and just before we left Lois strapped onto me a heavy pair of leather chaps. I would soon find out why. Of course, as it always is with trails, the beginning was deceptively easy and Gavilan was no exception. Lois in the lead, then myself, followed by Kimberly, another smart choice. Soon the horses began to labor, especially Charley, my steed.

The trail got steeper with increasing altitude and the horses labored, even more especially with a rider on their backs. All told, a physical challenge for them. The trail itself, with its steep drop-offs did little to settle the horses down, according to Kimberly, our lead wrangler. In fact, the trail was so narrow that before long the leather chaps over my legs were taking a beating from the trees lining the trail so tightly. With barely inches to spare, and with thousand foot drop-offs, this was no Sunday ride in the pasture. From time to time we had to stop, dismount and walk the horses up the trail, so they could catch their breath. It soon became necessary to loosen their cinches so that their chests could expand and bring more oxygen in, especially in this high altitude environment.

The saddles were now essentially just sitting on the horses backs, not well cinched in at all. While riding along my right leg hit a tree tight to the trail pretty hard. It pushed me and the saddle quickly hard to the left, so basically the saddle and I were sideways instead of atop the horse where I should have been. This position did not last long.

As I was falling free of the horse and saddle, I was going head first toward an impressive boulder, a coconut cracker. It all happened in slow motion as I remember it. My head about to meet the boulder when in literally the last instant Kimberly's hand came in to catch my noggin in a split second and just in time. My next line of defense, the rider's helmet. Fortunately it did not come to that.

The three of us and the horses were all a bit shaken up, a close call indeed. Better to fall to the inside of the trail than the outside with its steep drop offs. We walked the horses the rest of the way and still had to stop from time to time to let them catch their wind.

The meadow was beautiful, green, and fresh and there was the rock cairn that marked Larry's Memorial. The women rode on to the far side of the meadow. I knelt down, touched the earth, the warm stones, I pulled from my pocket a river stone I had engraved. I kissed the stone and left it in the rock pile. From my other pocket I pulled out the Jewish Mourner's Kaddish, I began....

Yit-ga-dal v'yit-ka-dash sh'me raba...finishing the prayer.

I left the stone and the written prayer behind in the memorial cairn and walked over to join the women for lunch. The trip down, much easier for the horses, was thankfully uneventful.

My goodbyes had been said, respect had been paid, "goodbye again," as sung by John Denver.

Brett, Jeff, Lucas

That next night we were celebrating Phyllis' seventieth birthday at a restaurant in town. Lucas, Larry's son and our physician, came by. The first words out of his mouth. "I see you went up to Gavilan Meadow by horseback to visit Pops." "Yes," I answered, "How did you know?" "A lot of horse tracks on the trail and the stone you left, 'See you on the other side.'" He continued,
"I read the Mourner's Kaddish in the still of the meadow."

We shared a drink and a sentiment. Life goes on.

Thanks to a horse named Charlie, and two wonderful women,
I experienced closure for my loss.

18

1977 2023

A SPECIAL MUSEUM LEADS TO A SPECIAL VISIT
The Tables Are Turned

As an artist or artisan, what you build, who your clients or audience are, whether you are represented by a gallery, an artists' co-op, or show your work from your home, studio, or work shop, having your work displayed in the Golden Goose would be museum recognition in my opinion.

Many years ago, at a friend's suggestion I applied to the Artful Home catalog to be represented by their catalog for home furnishings. I was quite impressed when the letter of my acceptance was signed by the former curator of the Smithsonian Museum.

Recently on a trip to San Diego we decided to visit the Mingei International Museum in Balboa Park. We had last visited about ten years ago and we were very impressed with the George and Mira Nakashima exhibit. Nearly an entire floor devoted to their work. After his passing in the 1990s, his daughter Mira took over the business. No small task, selecting trees worldwide for exquisite lumber, managing the multiple shops and craftsman, and working with the most discerning clients, private and corporate. A challenge indeed. I found Mira's work to be much like her father's but using more cherry wood and a feel to some pieces of being visually heavier.

Our first contact with George Nakashima's furniture was through a Philadelphia Inquirer newspaper article on his work and shop in New Hope, Pennsylvania, a nearby town. We were designing our first home and I had just finished building our dining room table, with large slabs of Brazilian rosewood. Having finished the rosewood table we needed chairs. I was smitten with Nakashima's Conoid chairs, first built for Nelson Rockefeller, the heir to Standard Oil, former Governor of New York and Vice President of the United States.

The chairs were expensive. The top of the line was crotch walnut, four chairs for $350 each. Phyllis was unsure about spending such a kingly sum in 1978, but having seen the chairs she recognized their value. After Nakashima's death in 1994, we found out that they were being sold at auction at antiquity pricing. Many years passed and we moved to New Mexico, the Land of Enchantment. While visiting a friend in Pennsylvania he invited us to meet his neighbor, a woodworker and Nakashima admirer. Jim, tall and distinguished, took us to his shop where he built exquisite antique reproductions.

He learned we had four Conoid chairs and commented on their value. I mentioned to him that the chairs, although authentic and we had the original invoice, were not signed. He asked me what was written on the bottom of the chairs. I said, "Hills 1 of 4" and so on. Upon hearing this he pinched my arm and said, "That is how he signed his chairs!"

He gave us a phone number to call and I spoke to John Sollo, the co-owner of the Auction House, Sollo Rago in New Jersey, which auctioned George Nakashima originals. After I took multiple pictures of the chairs, he called and told us they would be put in the coming auction for a minimum of $10,000 each, and that is just what they sold for at the hammer. I had one big problem, I no longer had my dining room chairs. At the time there were no published plans to buy, no secondary plans or instructions to see. Mr. Nakashima never published an article or woodworker's "how to" on building the Conoid chairs. They were seemingly a ghost chair and very secretive.

I still had our chairs and a month before I had to deliver them to Ft. Collins, Colorado, for their trip to New Jersey, I took one into the shop and painstakingly measured, traced, and fabricated the plywood forms, built templates and built models complete with joinery.

Finally, over many months I built six Conoid chairs to replace the four we sold. My chairs were built of Claro walnut (Western Oregon), of a higher aesthetic quality and even more so than the Pennsylvania black walnut used in the original Nakashima chairs. They were a success.

In July of 2023, we entered the Mingei Museum and went to the reception desk to buy our admission tickets. We began small talk and the folks at the desk noticed my hat, "The Taos Woodshop." As small talk segued to anecdotes of these stories, Devina (Visitor Experience Manager) asked if we would like to join her in the private library, furnished by Nakashima (Mira, I suspect). Of course we would.

After the door was opened and the lights turned on the beautiful furniture came into view. Classical live edge Walnut tables and of course Conoid chairs to compliment the tables. All from the studios of George and Mira Nakashima.

I told some of these same stories and explained construction details and techniques as well. Devina was duly impressed. After some contemplation, she invited me to examine the conference table in the Board Room, as there were complaints and issues concerning the new extensions on both ends of the table. She took us to the board room and the dining table, which ten years ago seated fourteen with Conoid chairs, had two new extensions (one on each end) and could now seat twenty-two.

The grain and finish on the extensions did not match the original table and they were dealing with complaints. Devina requested my observations and possible remedies. I sat down and wrote out an informal written report. I wrote up a series of steps to take in order improve the problems. I did it without judgment nor excessive criticism, you see, it was fifty years later, I was now in the position of the expert. The builder of the table's extensions was Mr. Nakashima's daughter, I treated her with her due respect. She made a mistake and could now right the wrong. Poetically speaking, the tables had turned, but with decency, compassion, and kindness. I also left my website and gallery contacts.

I was not sure where this would go. A few days later I received a letter from the Mengei International Museum. In part, thank you for visiting ... sharing your stories ... about your work ... about your experiences with George Nakashima ... as well as your expertise in the Nakashima style and construction. To be invited to give an expert opinion to a top Museum is an honor.

I am not sure I will have a piece exhibited in the Museum but I know for sure, that my talents and expertise were valued and appreciated by the Museum.

You see, there is an ironic twist to the story. In 1986, we hosted a Japanese exchange student, Hikaru, who became homesick. It occurred to me that inasmuch as Mr. Nakashima opened his home every Saturday morning to visitors, we would pay him a visit. Hikaru loved it, the tatami mats, Japanese screens, and the Nakashima family to speak to in his native language. I had with me beautiful and professional photographs of a multimedia oak roll top music cabinet with stained glass in each door, which I designed and built. I entered the cabinet into *Fine Woodworking Design Book II*, the best of design and craftsmanship in the United States. I showed the picture to Mr. Nakashima, but he did not particularly like the piece and a bit abrasively told me so. It turns out the piece did win a National Design Award from *Fine Woodworking* magazine and was in fact published in their *Design Book II* edition.

Talented man that George Nakashima was he could see only his work and his style, as he was more the oak tree than the willow.

Ten years ago, when my son bought his home, he requested a book matched cherrywood live edge dining table with five black ebony bow ties and Conoid seating for eight. As I tell this story my son has a picture of the original Nakashima table in the Mingei International Museum, a picture of me with two large cherrywood slabs, and, of course his completed table, so he gets to tell his story.

An unexpected, enjoyable and rewarding museum visit indeed! As Harry Chapin sang, "All my life's a circle."

Brett Hills table and chairs by Jeffrey Hills

The Epilogue to the Mingei Short Story

A few weeks later, after completing this Mingei Museum short story, I casually read an internet story on stained glass windows in a church. It triggered an immediate awareness of my own relationship to stained glass windows. The furniture piece, which I had shown to Mr. Nakashima and was my first major woodworking endeavor, it was a roll top music cabinet made of oak with two stained-glass doors. The stained glass scene on the roll top music cabinet was designed by a friend, Jerry Shurr.

It was a beautiful scene of Yellowstone Falls. We lived outside of Philadelphia, near Chestnut Hill. The yellow pages indicated that a stained glass studio was nearby, The Willet Stained Glass Studio. We went over and met E. Crosby Willet III. He reviewed the design and agreed on a price, which was way over my budget, but I just sensed in that dark and dusty workplace during the discussion of German glass for the greens, Italian for the pinks, French for the blues, that something special could happen. This was not paint by numbers.

After picking up the completed stained glass, it was time to install. In order to have the sky on top more illuminated than the lower *terra firma* portion, two aquarium lights were placed on top. On the bottom two forward facing angled mirrors were placed to reflect the diffuse light to the lower portion. The illuminated stain glass worked beautifully.

Professionally photographed by John Tuckerman and submitted to *Fine Woodworking* magazine, just before the deadline.

In due course I received a letter telling me of my accomplishment, national recognition and forth coming publication. Before I could pick up the two stain glass panels, Willet insisted on signing them with a diamond stylus. I could not understand why. It was only years later that I became aware of who E. Crosby Willet and family were:

1. The most famous church in the world, the Cathedral of Notre Dame in Paris, with the most prestigious stained glass artistry
   —repaired by the Willet family

2. The chapel at West Point
   —stained glass fabricated by the Willet family

3. The National Cathedral in Washington DC
   —stained glass fabricated by the Willet family

4. The chapel at the United Nations in New York City
   —stained glass fabricated by the Willet family

5. The Jeffrey Hills Roll Top Music Cabinet and Doors
   —stain glass fabricated by the Willet family, 1978

In hindsight I am not sure Mr. Nakashima would have a different opinion, but I am sure his daughter Mira would relate to my piece with more curiosity and mindfulness, whether it was her style or not. Perception is often preceded by "your." In fact, the time we live in, the choices we make, and the preferences we have all contribute to our world view. Mr. Nakashima was not wrong in his opinion, he was emotionally invested in his lens, his perceptions. Knowing that and respecting that, valuing the time he took to evaluate my work, I was inspired for a life time.

You can always or most always make the correct choice and it still may not equal success. The secret sauce is often luck. Being in the right place at the right time vs the wrong place at the wrong time. My best advice for success, "Chance favors the prepared mind." (Louis Pasteur).

You make your own luck. It's all likely going to even out, but if you can have a bit more good luck than bad, it is a good hand to play.

— **Jeffrey M. Hills**

As Kenny Rogers sang, "You have to know when to hold them and know when to fold them."

19 1968-Present

FOR THE FUN OF CARS
The Automobile Joining Design and Engineering

We all like to have fun and it is healthy for us as well. Cars, motorcycles, and all manner of the internal combustion engine, as well as today's electric drive trains, are essential for transportation, point A to point B. Almost from the beginning of the automotive age, evolutionary advancements began a ubiquitous and obvious march forward. From manual crank starting to the starting motor and twelve volt battery, mechanical improvements were on the march. From a stuffy cold and hot car to thermostatically controlled heaters and air conditioners. Always a march of engineering, performance, comfort and luxury.

Although I loved cars and sure needed one to get to and from school, it became obvious that cars do not fall out of the trees.

The joy of this chapter is to share with you how some special cars came my way. There was some luck involved, but definitely a good concept of what exceptional design and engineering looked like.

After years of saving, I bought my first car, a used 1966 Volvo B18 122, Amazon in cream white with rounded head lights and rounded front fenders. I bought the car in the spring of 1968. It was a soft classic in the making. They still sell well and a collector version was owned by General Colin Powell.

85

A four speed buggy whip stick shift, a plain and simple dash, comfortable seats, and the first manufacturer to include three-point seat belts as standard equipment.

The engine compartment was straight forward, with lots of room. As basic a set up as you could have for a beginner to learn sixties' mechanics.

The one challenge was getting the twin carbs in sync with their air flow. A synchronizer that measured positive air flow was the trick to matching the twin carbs up.

Comedian Jerry Seinfeld on his show, "Comedians in Cars Getting Coffee," said, "The Volvo-ness, this car is the essence of great sixties Swedish values: honest, hard working, unfussy, not out to impress and built to last."

I totally loved the car and began itching for a Volvo sports car, the P1800. It was not in the cards and probably for the better, as our son was entering the picture and this was not a "family" car, not at all. I still enjoy seeing the beautiful lines of the P1800.

A bit of Volvo and automotive history. Irv Gordon, from New York City, holds the world record for the most miles driven in a single car, clocking 3.2 million miles in a Volvo P1800.

A BMW, the first of many, 600/5 motorcycle became my ride in 1970. Black and white pipping for the seats, opposing cylinder heads in the classic BMW arrangement. Be it rain, snow, or cold, it was my

ride to school and work. Phyllis had a car for her and baby Brett. The Beemer also took Phyllis and myself to Williams, Arizona, and to many National Parks for an exceptional 1973 adventure trip out West. I continued to use it for primary commutes until 1975 when our daughter Rachael was born.

The Volvo 122 was sold in 1972. We bought a Toyota Land Cruiser FJ40 short back. This very boxy 4X4 in sky blue would be our ride out West in 1972. Toyota's FJ40 was essentially a short wheel base off-road 4X4 with a manual shift and locking hubs. It was as rugged as they came. Amenities, none, absolutely none. A friend gifted me a tape deck and Janis Joplin, played over and over which was most appreciated. It had a three-speed manual transmission, mated to a 3.9 liter, 6-cylinder engine. We outfitted the back seat area with a foam mattress which only worked with the rear doors opened. We bought it for about the mid two thousands. Mint today would be eighty thousand. One of many winners: engineering, design, low numbers built and luck. Although quite serviceable for our western trip, it was no match for the cobble stone streets of Philadelphia. Jerry Seinfeld's take, "I have always liked these vehicles. It is basic, it is classic, it is durable, it is user friendly."

Right after dental school I saw a nice looking Porsche on a local mechanic's lot in Germantown. As best as I can remember it was a Porsche 356B hard top coupe in battle ship gray, my first sports car. The cabriolet 356 of my "fav," Janis Joplin. Her estate left it to her brother who recently sold it for five million dollars. Provinance can play an important part in selling prices.

It was an air cooled engine making 70 hp. With dual carbs. As often happens in life, the Porsche became an unaffordable luxury as we were settling into our first home. I spent about two thousand on it, and today the average selling price according to classic.com is $76,000.

Of course a top cabriolet model, excellent condition and low miles can go for near a million. Once again low miles and low numbers built. Jerry Seinfeld, "A Rusty Car in the Rain." "This is my car. I use it to go places, run errands, take people around, or drive it just for the sheer unbelievable fun of it. A subtle sophistication, so elegant and complex in the curves of the body."

I was thinking, maybe it is time for a family car, but perhaps a bit sporty. In 1974 I was in luck. The BMW dealer nearby had some really beautiful, sporty cars. Per the 1972 issue of *Car and Driver,* "The BMW 2002 tii, exquisite performance for the unrehabilitated car addict. No matter how hard you try, you can not help but like it. It is the essence of motoring truth, just finely honed machinery and fuel injected to make the person breath hard."

After chatting with the dealer representative for a while he suggests we go for a ride. Nothing exotic on the design of the body, the interior was all black with clean VDO instruments and a four speed on the floor. I got behind the wheel and fifty plus years later, I am still behind the wheel of a BMW, although different ones all along the way. The ride was breath taking, speed and handling in perfect balance, synergy defined. A relatively light car but fast with fuel injection and large exhausts. The 140 bhp engine seemed to get stronger the higher in the band curve you pushed it. It handled exceptionally well relative to its power. I enjoyed breaking road contact with the rear end and then getting it back in line. This was a driver's car especially when the family was not aboard. I loved the car and the Fjord Blue color until we decided to move up to a BMW 528i, 6-cylinder fuel injected, much more power, a touch less handling. Perhaps it was like going from a sports sedan to a sporty sedan. It cost about $4,000 for the 2002 tii car in 1974, the top sale for the tii to date according to classic.com, is $100,800. With an average sale price of $30,000, Jerry Seinfeld noted, "The 1972 BMW 2002 tii, stroke out on a hot machine, this was one of the first cars in America in the 1960s that made people think, 'Hey maybe these Germans are kind of fun in a certain way.'" Low numbers, superb engineering and performance. It will always be a top car for me.

Time to build a house again so maybe we needed a work vehicle, maybe the cool looking 1975 Ford Bronco, boxy in blue body and white top, bought used in 1978 for roughly $1,500. It had a Ford V8 302 cubic inch engine, rated at 125 hp. It was the perfect vehicle to have while we built our home in Gwynedd Valley. The access road was dirt, mud, and quite rutted. A 4X4 was a necessity. It also had ample storage in the back for tools and supplies. All in all, just right for that time in our life. Recent sales for pristine top vehicles $210,000–$260,000. For average sales $50,000–$75,000 will get you one. Interestingly, both Toyota on its Land Cruiser and Ford on its Bronco did reprisals recently. You cannot keep a great vehicle down. Of note: the BMW 600/5 series of the early 1970s motorcycle as well as the Volvo P1800 have both been brought back as modern versions of the originals.

As we settled into our new home I reminisced about a fun college friend, Steve Engle, who had an Austin Healy 3000 when we were in Hofstra University in the mid to late 1960s. He used to give me lifts home as I had no vehicle of my own. One time I was for some reason taking my cat cadaver home from my comparative anatomy class. Steve forbade me from keeping the cat in its formaldehyde drenched plastic bag inside the car. So for the ten mile drive to my home I held the cat outside the car, for sure a lot of dirty looks, but no cat calls. This sports car was a gem. Absolutely beautiful. I said to myself, "Someday."

Well it was 1983 and someday had arrived, I began looking. I found a local Austin Healy 1967 3000 BJ8 MKIII, the last model and the most refined model built. I test drove it and bought it on the spot for $2,300. This car needed work, luckily I loved the car so we were in it for the long haul. Parts and pieces were readily available and I had a dental patient, Dave, who was an ace mechanic and we both agreed to a barter arrangement. His and his familiy's care for me and my car's care.

Every winter the car went to Dave with a list of work goals. Every spring I picked the car up and enjoyed it, top down for the summer. This went on for twenty years until we moved out West and I sold the car, title in hand, tears in my eyes to a nice guy from Pittsburgh, Pennsylvania, who offered me life time visitation.

The Austin Healy began its history in the 1950s as the 100/4-BN1 and BN2. The BN1 set a record at the Utah Salt Flats going 109 miles per hour. The Healy evolved over two decades.

The mighty Healy 3000, 1967, BJ8, MK III, the last year in production and the most advanced. From plastic windows to roll-up windows, from four cylinder to six cylinder, 3000 cc, 148 Hp., 165 foot pounds of torque. Another rule; a car's first year production runs as well as the car's last year production are the best. Our personal upgrades were many, including larger tires to better fill the wheel wells with seventy-eight spoke knock off wheels. New seats and carpeting. All rust removed, parts replaced and appropriate welding. A custom maple burl dash was installed. The Lucas, unreliable electronics replaced by those of Allison and Bosch for reliable starts and tow-free trips.

It is one thing to own a collectible car, but it is quite another to use it as an everyday drive. Knowing it was my go-to drive was my favorite part. No decision based on the weather, just get in and go.

Other work done included carburation, engine, trans, and clutch. Actually pretty much an on frame reconstruction. One spring, after much of the work had been done, I went to pick up the car.

Unbeknownst to me Dave painted the car British Racing Green ... a beautiful job. I was surprised and pleased until the rainy weather started. I found myself worrying about the weather now. In the early days of ownership the floor pans were rusted out. I would keep the top down as it was a hassle to close it. The rain came, and drained, then the sun came out and I would drive it home. Usually the tonneau half cover was in place for at least some weather protection. Now with all the rust removed, new seats, carpets and paint I would check the weather before I went out. The worm had turned. The carefree days were over. No more cat hanging out the window, no more "Let it rain," who cares attitude. A loss of innocence or at least "car innocence."

Graham Robson the author of *The Big Healy* concludes, "In every way, indeed, the Big Healy was a classic, a thoroughbred machine and no famous car can have a better epitaph than that."

Jerry Seinfeld quipped, "Mad men in a death machine. This is a car if you want to say, I really love British sports cars and dammit I will go down with one if I have to."

I bought the car in 1983 for $2,300 and sold it in 2003 for $23,000. One of the most pristine 3000' on the classic market recently sold for $400,800 at Pebble Beach Auctions. A nice one can be had for $50,000–$75,000.

I was honored when my British Racing Green BJ8 Austin Healy 3000 MK III came in First in Class at the Reading (Pennsylvania) Sports Car Show.

It is a given that cars depreciate but I would say not always, a testament to my British Racing Green (BRG) Austin Healy 3000. Once more, low numbers, convertible, and excellent condition.

Moving onto the 1980s requires stopping off in the 1950s. A car, strikingly beautiful, the iconic BMW 507 Roadster designed by Albrecht Von Goertz, working under Max Hoffman, President of BMW Motor Corporation. The 507 was

sold between 1956 and 1959. Only 252 were sold and only 202 remain today. It had eight cylinders pumping out 150 hp. The original price tag was about $5,000, significantly the highest price hammered at auction recently was $5,000,000—jaw dropping, but soft top, extremely low numbers built, fast, and in concours condition.

The lines, the elegance and performance has stood the test of time. Why is all this automotive history so special to me? Who was Goertz and why does it matter to me and the automotive world? The 507 did not sell well, 252, but it created the BMW brand of which I have bought into thirteen times over 55 years. I was too young and economically challenged to own a BMW 507 but decades later I owned two BMW Z-3s, a 2000 and 2001 respectively, inspired by Goertz's 507. The photos will clearly illustrate the design similarities and pedigree. In the mid 1980s I owned an American muscle car built originally by Studebaker, the Avanti.

Raymond Loewy, a renowned designer, had a chance meeting in 1940 with Goertz in the parking lot of the Waldorf Astoria hotel in New York City. They hit it off and Loewy sent Goertz to a design college in California and gave him a job in the Studebaker studio in Indiana shortly thereafter. Goertz's design philosophy emphasized the marriage of form and function. Look beautiful, drive beautifully, build practical and engaging vehicles to drive.

One of my three favorite cars to drive, the BMW Z3 with a six cylinder, 2.8 liter, 193 hp., mated to a five-speed manual transmission. The shifts were fast and the 6.3 seconds to 60 mph were quite engaging. Rear wheel drive was also refreshing, given today's all wheel drive cars. The front grill, the side grill, the rear wheel fender haunches, very muscular. It had enough power for spirited driving, but not enough power to get you in trouble, too easily.

The Z3 was one of several BMWs that was a direct desendent of Goertz's work with BMW on the 507.

The most awarded car I have ever owned was the 1974 Avanti in sky blue. Reading Henning's Auto Collectibles, I noticed the ads for the Avantis. They were drivable, affordable, and collectible.

I found one in Ft. Lauderdale, Florida, and on a family trip to Florida looked it over. A car hauler delivered it to my office in Pennsylvania. The Avanti was designed by Raymond Loewy, Goertz's mentor, in forty-one days. Andy Granatelli of STP fame was in charge of powering the Avanti back in 1962. Studebaker advertised its Avanti as, "the world's fastest production car," with a top speed of 178 mph, even faster then a Ferrari 250 GTO (174 mph). There was a slower version, which was the one I owned. A four barrel 289 cubic inch, V8 engine, pushing out 240 hp. The interior and exterior were luscious and functional. My high point with the car was winning Best in Class at the New Hope Auto Show.

I eventually sold the Avanti for just what I bought it for, $26,000. Today the last Avanti sold at auction went for $49,990.

In the mid 1970s while sitting close to the stage at Valley Forge Music Theater in the round, while enjoying an Alice Cooper concert, Phyllis was invited on stage to dance with an impromptu group of women. So you may wonder... Alice Cooper's favorite car—the Studebaker Avanti, small world. I will pass on the makeup.

Raymond Loewy is listed as the world's third most famous designer:

- The Avanti
- The Coca Cola Logo
- The Bullet Train
- Graphics and logos for Exxon, Shell, and the US Post Office

He is known as the man who designed everything. He also set Alfred Von Gertz on to his automotive design path. Which in turn opened the world to the BMW Automobile. The Z3 and Z8 were direct descendants of his design work.

Seinfeld said, "Everybody respects a bloody nose. Studebaker did not go well so in a last ditch effort to save that business, they asked design genius Raymond Loewy to make them a sports car which he did in a forty-day crash program on the outskirts of Las Vegas."

One of the cars I have truly enjoyed with my eye for design is the Avanti, "move forward" in Italian, one of my all time favorites.

After my enjoyable stint with the Avanti we were introduced in France to the Mercedes Benz 190E 2.3 L, which sold in the United States as a Cosworth built 16 Valve 2.3L. A Mercedes muscle car, making 207 bhp with a five-speed manual transmission. Only 1,880 were imported to North America and I signed up for one in 1987. It was black on black with a nice splash of wood trim and shift console, esthetics befitting a Benz. With four valves per cylinder, fuel injection and high compression ratios, engines were putting out horse power like never before. This was a fun car to drive the mountain twisties; it could also take you to the symphony on a Saturday night. The German doorman at the Grand Hyatt Hotel in New York City gave me a strong smile and a thumbs up upon our arrival for a New York City visit. The top selling price at auction $51,888. Of note, exceptional engineering dressed up as a Mercedes Benz.

Home building, furniture crafting, Airstream towing all need a work horse. For the last twenty years it has been Ford F-150s, F-150 King Ranch and an F-250. Since 2014 it has been a Ford F-150, 6.2 liter engine, 411 hp., super cab. The engine has normal air aspiration, which means it is a non-turbo power plant. This 2014 was the end of an era.

The last steel body F-150 built. As our Airstreams grew bigger, modifications were made to the F-150 to help make our way through the mountains more doable, while towing 6,500 pounds in high altitudes.

- K and N cold air intake filter.
- Electronic chipping for increased power as well as gas mileage.
- Heavy duty front brakes for help going down the mountain passes.
- Auxiliary transmission cooler for help getting up and over those same mountain passes, without over heating.
- Over all, a commendable working vehicle, sometimes just what is needed, especially in rural America.

My favorite cars and trucks, all sharing performance, exterior aesthetics, and interior luxury as appropriate. I rarely bought with investment in mind, but there have been ample surprises. Although I had an eye for cars, I think luck played into each vehicle's success. It is just not possible to know where the market place will be in twenty years. Further more, the fun is in the experience not in the projected value. If you can enjoy your automotive experience, that is of paramount importance. The numbers and current value is just a data driven optic to justify the story line. My advice, I try to buy used when possible with warranties and avoid like the plague first year models.

20 2024

TODAY

I have worked hard, I have accomplished

much and have enjoyed this life. As my own Philadelphian, Linda Creed, wrote and Whitney Houston sang, "I decided long ago never to walk in anyone's shadow. If I fail, if I succeed, at least I will live as I believe."

My inspiration for decades. I have probably walked in my share of shadows. Probably many have walked in my shadow. Many have helped me and I know I have helped many. If you live long enough, you realize you have not figured it all out, your frailties and fallibilities are still dancing in your head and weighing on your body. It is good to know you gave it your best and had fun doing it. You will even have learned, if you are fortunate enough, the meaning of Kahlil Gibran's words, "work is love made visible."

For all the people in my life, for the adventures, and for the meaningful work, I am truly grateful. Of course and with pleasure and pride I have always said that my secret weapon has been my wife of fifty-five years, Phyllis. She is a unique blend of smarts, high energy, and a witty and charming personality. Now that is a secret weapon, indeed. Whether building a stone wall, navigating in a storm, kayaking down the raging white waters of the Rio Grande River, or helping to glue up and sand a table top. Riding on horses, motor cycles or sports cars, you can count on Phyllis to add to the experience. When the adventure begins, she will be just the asset you need. She is calm and cool and collected under the most trying of circumstances. So as always, a heartfelt thank you to my loving wife, Phyllis.

Today I still live as I have for the last twenty years just north of Taos, New Mexico. I live off a dirt road, Rock Garden Gully. The winters are long and cold. We split our firewood and most of it gets cut in half on the outside band saw, so that it can fit in our wood stove, which is small. I work in the shop, preparing furniture for the Gallery's busy season.

I am nursing my share of aches and pains that people my age deal with. However, I do continue to cross country ski, swim, bike ride, and kayak down the Rio Grand River. I enjoy open fire cooking with the prunings from my apple trees. My orchard, apple, pear, plum, and peach yields us plenty of fresh fruit to eat, freeze and share. Our dog Duke, at the age of thirteen, still runs free out back on our trails. He is a big hearted black Lab, Great Dane mix who does not know his age, but always finds his way home.

Our son Brett, a commercial realtor lives in the North Valley of Albuquerque, 120 miles south of us. His lovely home sports a lap pool, for my swims and a sitting pool for his Mom to read in, covered by a wide umbrella. He winters in Taos Ski Valley, which enables him to work and enjoy skiing from his mountain side abode.

He is an excellent skier who is often seen on the covers of various ski magazines and a true ambassador of Taos Ski Valley. It is also nice having him nearby.

Our daughter, Rachael and husband, Brett live west of Denver in Lakewood, Colorado. Rachael enjoys her career as a dental hygienist and educator. She is an exercise enthusiast. Her husband Brett was for many years the owner/chef of the Wooden Table restaurant in Denver. My favorite is when he prepares an incredible meal for the family and slices off a preview for me to taste, lovely. They share their home with their children, our grandchildren Olivia, born in 2010, and Sam, born in 2012. Olivia loves cooking and baking. I taught Olivia the basics of ice skating and recently she enrolled in a formal ice skating class. Sam is, as we are, proud of his recently earned black belt and being an assistant instructor at his Taekwondo center. We all get together regularly but must watch the weather as travel in winter especially through the high mountain passes can be a challenge.

Although I miss much about my life back East, especially boating on the Chesapeake Bay, I have loved these past twenty years living in a small rural town in the shadow of 13,000-foot mountain peaks. We technically live in rural America but at the edge of the frontier. There are not many places where my career as a woodworker could have taken off and afforded me terrific opportunities. Taos is a very artistic community and seventy-five miles to the South, Santa Fe represents a world class art market.

I am still with Michael Galya at his Gallery on Canyon Road in Santa Fe. Delivering new pieces for the Gallery gives us a chance to enjoy a day trip in Santa Fe. Seeing friends, fine restaurants and shopping affords us opportunities we do not have in Taos.

In my spare time I enjoy reading, music, daily exercise and yoga. This year 2024 Phyllis and I will celebrate 55 years of marriage. It is everything a good marriage should be including, "doing the work." We vacation at home in the winter with five ski areas for cross-country, downhill, and snow biking. There is no need to travel in the winter, as we are living at home and short drives for any outdoor snow activity. Come summer we enjoy four to five weeks in Breckenridge, Colorado, where for sixteen years we have Airstreamed at Tiger Run RV Resort. We especially enjoyed having our kids and grandchildren join us.

Although we recently sold our Airstream we will still summer in Breckenridge which, at 8,500 feet, is about ten degrees cooler than Taos. These days it is much less work for us to rent a home and have plenty of room for all of us. Nearby there is Lake Dillon, where the group likes to paddle board, and Phyllis, Duke and I enjoy the kayak. The Breckenridge bike paths (55miles) are excellent, connecting a handful of terrific towns for lunch or a cool drink.

I have enjoyed my work on the Boards of Child-Rite Special Needs Adoption Agency, Rocky Mountain Youth Corps, and, currently, our Road Association. I do road maintenance with my Kubota tractor from time to time. Where else but in Taos?

I continue to read prolifically, all the while feeling quite knowledgeable and wise. While walking on our trails recently, in the stillness and bright sunshine, I can hear one of my favorites by Joni Mitchell: "I've looked at life from both sides now, from win and lose and still somehow, It is life's illusions I recall, I really don't know life at all."

In my twenties as a lonely, hardworking freshman dental student, I would play the Judy Collins version over and over after classes in the afternoon. The school work was difficult, I was missing Phyllis, the apartment was a dump without furniture. After twenty minutes of "Both Sides Now," I forgot the day; I relaxed and began the evening studies.

Today, while walking on the trails I know I have lived my best life for sure, but now I know what wisdom is, the lessons life has taught me and I am overwhelmed with gratitude and appreciation as I see my life in the rear view mirror, both fulfillment and losses. And yes, I am wise enough to say as Joni Mitchell wrote, there is still the sense there is more to learn, more to experience. That, "I really don't know life at all." And so another day, another step forward.

The journey from seven decades ago when my cousin Michael gifted me my first book, *The Book of Wonder* to authoring this book, "Who would have thought?" It truly is a "wonder."

Part II

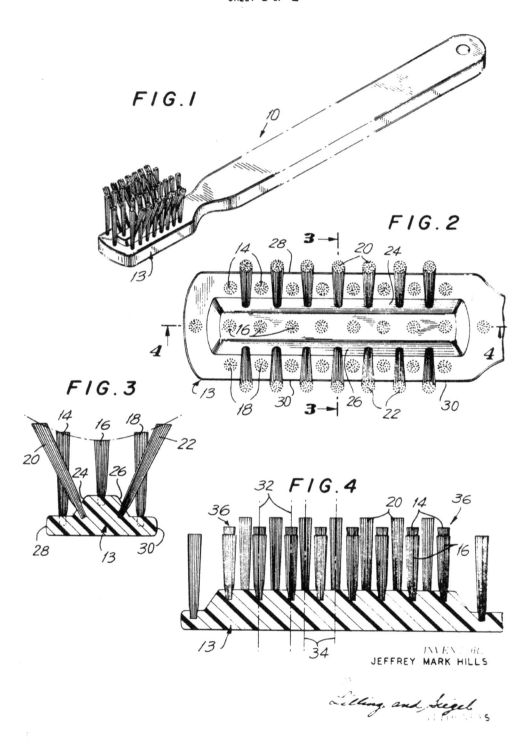

1969, 1973, 1990, Present

Patent Number 3,722,020

"Toothbrush with concavity formed by bristle ends." So reads Patent 3,722,020, awarded the 1971 American Dental Association Scientific Achievement Award. This toothbrush is represented in the American Dental Association National Museum, Baltimore, Maryland.

Ponder this, you buy a lottery ticket, eleven digits. You are home reading off the winning numbers. You miss the ten million dollar payout by one digit, of one number. How any individual deals with it is his own story. Being an inventor means you put in work, perhaps mechanics, engineering, and creative energy into something novel.

Unless you work for a corporation, you will be up against the corporate world, financial pressure, building the new "mouse trap," differentiating it from prior art, racing to beat potential competitors, filing with the United States Patent Office and other patent offices around the world, and facing many other counter forces and headwinds. Daunting to say the least.

An inventor should be an expert and at least work in his field of art. My fields would be dental, medical, and woodworking. I have invented in all three fields.

This story of my life as an inventor can take two paths. An inventor at work or the financial struggles with the potential winning lottery number. I will focus on what has had the most meaning for me, which is the former.

The inventor thinks laterally and literally, one and one makes three.
— KENNETH A. BROWN, *Inventors at Work*, 1988

How does one and one make three? Because between the first "one" and the second "one" a surprise takes place, an "aha" moment occurs. Intuitiveness and creativity jump a synapse in the neurophysiology of the mind. The end result, a creative moment. Has it been done anywhere else in the world before or concurrently? Will it fulfill the criteria of a legally binding invention? Will you persevere, work, and spend the necessary money on models (prototypes), applications, and attorneys in hopes of being awarded a patent? If not, then it is an idea, perhaps a very good idea. And there it remains. Through the years many people have come to me with ideas. I have never seen one develop into a patent.

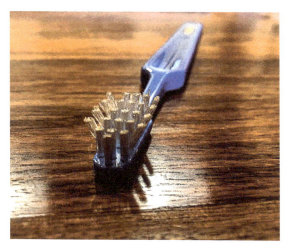

What makes an inventor tick? There is, as Edison observed, the desire "to find a better way." When I, as a sophomore dental student, sat in class while oral hygiene (essentially tooth brushing) was being taught, my one thought was, "There has to be a better way." I began mindfully to create a future, a better way. When I was first in practice I would refer on average of forty patients per year to the specialty of periodontology. When I retired thirty years later only a handful of patients were referred. Home care, flossing, brushing, rinsing became, as the French would say "habituel." My new and novel toothbrush was awarded the American Dental Association Scientific Achievement Award in 1971.

The insight I had was to make brushing effectively easier and more efficient. To make it easier you had to take a giant meta physical step. The past history of toothbrushes addressed and appropriately so, cleaning of the teeth, essentially plaque removal. That was important. Even more important was cleaning the dental or periodontal sulcus. That area from the top edge of the gum line to the bottom where the gum reattaches to the tooth. This space is usually one to three millimeters in a healthy mouth. More than three millimeters can possibly indicate a periodontal pathological condition.

The anatomical word, sulcus, had never been introduced or used in a prior toothbrush patent, therefore new and novel, a giant step taken.

My patented toothbrush was awarded ten claims. Claim number two states, "A toothbrush according to claim 1, wherein said substantially perpendicular row of bristles comprises and at least one of said oblique rows of bristles comprising means for cleaning sulcus tooth areas."

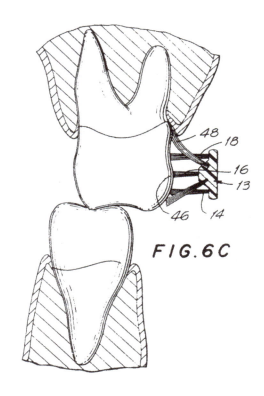

In 2019 World Daily Holding was the thirty-ninth largest market capitalized company ($245 billion) in the world. They are Asia and the world's largest manufacturer of toothbrushes (yes, even for prominent American companies). They have as recently as 2019 and as early as 2016, cited my Patent 3,722,020 nine times. You can see their "Better Toothbrush or "V Max Toothbrush" on Amazon. A patent is protected for seventeen years, plus patent pending. It is then in the public domain. Although you cannot have an exact copy, as there is no novelty, you can use various elements and be awarded a six digit design patent. World Wide did not deal with the small engineering details. Perhaps close enough is good enough. Before 3,722,020 Patent Hills, there were four toothbrush patents that were in the field of art and that the United States Patent Office deemed necessary to cite. Subsequent to Hills 3,722,020 as of January 11, 2024, there are seventy-two patent applications that cited Hills Patent #3,722,020.

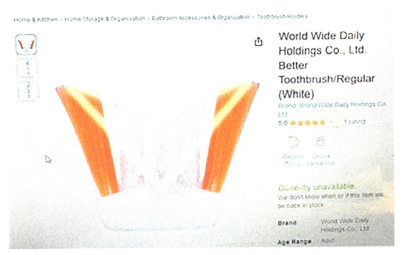

105

Some prominent companies that cited and used my Patent art include Colgate-Palmolive Company, Cheesebrough-Ponds USA, Gillette, Inc., The Procter and Gamble Company, Braun GmbH, Water Pik, Inc., and World Wide Daily Holdings Company.

My toothbrush, Hills 3,722,020 was granted its patent on March 27, 1973. Seventeen years and two days later, on March 29, 1990, Procter &Gamble received their design patent and began manufacturing their abridged version of my toothbrush—two days after the expiration. No small coincidence but keep in mind that twenty one years after my aha moment of creation, my moment was still extremely relevant. For World Wide Holdings, the concept and the brush mechanics are still relevant forty-seven years later. What iPhone model could say that? My insight on how to clean the sulcus and the new way of looking at an old problem has stood the test of time.

The invention is but one part of an inventor's journey. In my particular situation, having earned a dental degree and desiring to practice dentistry, the option of selling the toothbrush outright or even better licensing it to a company and taking a percentage would be most preferable. My last choice would be to build it and distribute it myself. Enormous sums of money and time would be needed which would marginalize my four years of work earning a dental degree, and certainly my growing family's financial security.

The inventor must have curiosity.

As always, the inventor must have curiosity. How does this work? Can it be better? I found myself driven. After disappointments I would be even more driven. The more difficult the task, the more interested and passionate I became. I have always liked the four "P's"—Purpose, Passion, Perseverance, and Persistence. When we say inventor the implication is all the neuroscience that goes into what we call creativity or intuitiveness. The mechanics and engineering to build it. All the emotional intelligence to deal with the ups and downs. At last, if you ever get this far, the legal and business knowledge and skills needed by the armful.

My first patent, the toothbrush, followed the usual steps. Apply for the patent, do battle with the United States Patent Office, be awarded your patent, then go forth and try to sell or license your patent. As a matter of course you would need marketing, prototypes, promotional material, and perhaps studies on efficacy as well.

My next four inventions would see a different and more dollar efficient strategy. Provisional patent applications filed. Marketing data and prototypes in hand. Contact prospective buyers as soon as possible. If successful then your ticket is punched. If unsuccessful then thousands saved on legal and patent fees.

I believe that woodworking is closer to art and craftsmanship and inventing is closer to engineering while being pushed by curiosity. They do share at their very inception intuitiveness and the creative moment. The instantaneous flash, the spontaneity of that creative design moment, it is almost breathless in its effect on the body. A flood of dopamine, if you will.

I tend to see objects and pictures as three dimensional representations in my mind. This typically occurs upon waking, at any hour. The trick is to get it on paper as best you can, the details can be worked out during the waking hours.

First, I curiously think about the problem, then go to sleep, let the subconscious percolate or make its synapse connections. So yes, one plus one can equal three.

Being creative is a wonderful quality but as an inventor creativity is very much intertwined with purpose and an engineered end point. It must fulfill the definition of an invention and fulfill the requirements of a utility patent.

To be regarded as an invention, an idea needs to include an inventive step. An inventive step must be non-obvious. That is it would not readily occur to an expert in the relevant technology or field. There are four requirements an invention must meet in order to receive a utility patent.

• Ability to be used; it can work and not be just a theory

• A clear description of how to make and use the invention

• New or novel (something not done before)

• "Not obvious" as related to a change to something already invented.

It is probable that inventors are born, and it is possible to educate, motivate and nurture the creative process. As Louis Pasteur said, "Chance prefers the prepared mind."

Often times a "need" is conceptualized. Sometimes this "need" is desperately pursued which supports the old adage, "Desperation is the mother of invention."

When I decided to pursue a second invention, I was by then expecting to fail but I believed I could succeed. I was driven by the pure joy of the creative process. I would go from an idea in my mind, to a picture in my mind, to a drawing, to a working model in my hand. The process made me happy. I felt content and joyful.

So, who is an inventor, who am I? I speak of the creative and intuitive process. Neil Diamond sings of the "solitary man." Invention is a very lonely art.

On one hand you conceive of an invention and you become the champion. Are you chasing success or are you chasing a rainbow? What if you are ahead of your time or problematically too far ahead of the invention. I will explain the storied fifty-year history of my toothbrush.

As an inventor you have a built-in bias. It is your skin in the game, but your saving grace may very well be in the answer you have to the question, "How much confidence do you have in your intuition?" Everyone likes to think he/she is right. Before you sink your time and treasure into an idea, you would do well to know you are right and for good measure, know where the off ramp is. No one is perfectly "right" all the time.

My inventions seem to be simple and clear mechanical devices. If it has purpose and is beautiful, I see it as elegant; there is a beauty in elegance.

One must see problems, nurture ideas, solve, care, invent as appropriate and as needed. Be as the child, let your brain play, let those circuits run wild. You may be surprised at the results.

When building, whether relationships, furniture, or a brick wall, my rule of thumb is that first row of bricks must be plumb, level, and true. That is your starting point, start true.

There are two stories for every invention. The patent story and how it was built. Second, the marketing and business side. I will begin at the very beginning, a good place to start.

108

After taking a class in brushing technique for patients, it became obvious that the instructor kept repeating, "Hold the brush at a forty-five degree angle to the tooth and gum." It sounds pretty straight forward until you realize:

- There is an upper and lower dentition.
- There is a right and left side.
- There is an outer and inner aspect.

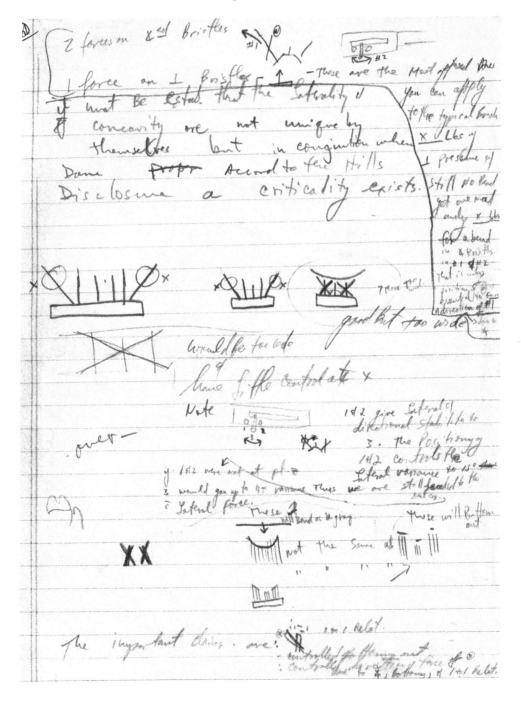

A sense of purpose and direction as well as dexterity would be needed. My first thought, there has to be an easier, more effective way. The wheels began to turn, the night time synapses were working in overtime. I kept pads and pencils everywhere. As I would draw a toothbrush, I would improve my drawing as I would apply it to the anatomy of the dentition. As the drawings evolved it very much became an exercise in architect Louis H. Sullivan's, "Form follows function." Curves with both concave aspects and its compliment of convex aspects began to synergize the project three dimensionally. (See patent pages at the end of this chapter.)

The reading of the patent follows the usual pattern:

- Drawings

- Abstract

- Background

- Summarys

- Brief description of the drawings

- Description of the preferred embodiment

- The claims

When reading the patent, it is easy to get lost in its technical patent "speak." I will break it down to a version for better understanding and appreciation. For simplicity, consideration of other forms, designs or iterations that are covered by the mechanical patent, will not be discussed but can be assumed to function in the same mechanical fashion. To the claims I will interject my addendum to the pending patent submitted January 18, 1972.

The head of the toothbrush is formed by five rows of bristles across and a compliment of longitudinal rows. This is the **Theory of the Box**: there is an optimum size for a toothbrush that satisfies biological needs and the size of this box seeks to satisfy these biological needs.

The bristles generally form a concave plane, the **Theory of Concavity**: there is an optimum concavity which conforms to the average convexity of an average tooth face.

There is an outer row of bristles that extend outward at approximately forty five degrees and extend beyond the vertical height of the inner three rows of bristles, the **Theory of Arcuate Motion**.

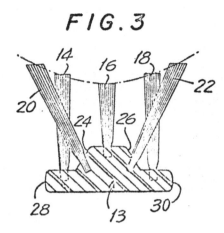

FIG. 3

Hills Toothbrush Cross Section

Theory of Arcuate Motion

As 20 above increases the potential arcuate motion increases.

As 20 above decreases the potential arcuate motion decreases.

As 14 moves toward the leading edge of 20 the arcuate motion decreases.

As 14 moves away from the leading edge of 20 the arcuate motion increases.

Claim number seven, wherein the toothbrush engages the sulcus to clean and with minimal chance of damage to the gingivae and its attachment fibers, this relates directly to the theory of Arcuate Motion.

Theory of Flexure

As 20 increases in relation to 14,16,18 the potential flexure of these bristles increases.

As 20 decreases in relation to 14,16,18 the potential flexure of these bristles decreases.

Zero degrees of # 20 or ninety degrees of angle of # 20 would imply no ability for # 20 to flex into the sulcus, therefore forty-five degrees +/- will work.

It follows that the three inner rows help from the concavity and help to control the direction and distance of "travel" of the outer row 20.

Gratefully, using the toothbrush does not require as much effort as engaging with a United States Patent Office examiner.

After I had drawings in hand I took a train to Virginia, and visited the United States Patent Office. Today you can do all the necessary searches on line with a computer, from your office or home. In the early 1970s it was a road or train trip. With an early train out of Philadelphia and a late train out of Virginia, I had a day to find and explore the field of art, toothbrushes, and see if my idea had been done—was it patentable? It was a day well spent, we were onto something.

Through my uncle, an attorney, I contacted the patent law firm of Lilling and Siegel in New York City.

The patent process began:
- Application
- Rejection
- Arguments
- Amendments
- Fewer Rejections
- Further Arguments
- Acceptance
- Patent Issued

Simultaneously, I began building a workable prototype. I built the original prototype using bristles from an off the shelf brush. The plastic handle was formed and fashioned with denture acrylics, so we had a denture handle with recycled bristles. With something of a prototype in hand, I made more detailed drawings and met with a professional model maker in New Jersey. They made a representational prototype with blue plastic handles and the bristles were actually represented by a round composite mini rods. Upon my approval negative rubber molds were made. The bristles could easily, accurately and repeatedly be placed and then acrylic could be poured and cured.

Once the patent pending was issued, there was at least a modicum of protection and that would afford me enough protection to marginalize the need for a nondisclosure agreement. As a matter of course most companies would not ever consider signing an NDA. Their reasoning, the product may currently be in research, in house.

A pilot study was done by Temple University clinical instructor, Dr. Murray Cohen and published in the juried Journal of Periodontology, 1973, 44:183. The study using plaque dyes proved the toothbrush was more effective than a conventional toothbrush.

From the Public Library trade journals, a list was made of all relevant companies. An introductory letter was sent out.

Interest dribbled in. This was the early 1970s, there were no personal computers, there were no Xerox copy machines. There was nothing easy about this, especially for a student and his wife.

The most interest was from Bristol Myers, headquartered in Manhattan. They sent me a letter of intent, which was a great first step, but shortly thereafter a less inviting letter was received.

- The Newark, New Jersey Brush Company could not build the brush at a reasonable price. Its machinery was not computerized nor mechanically adaptable for such a project.
- Bristol Myers' legal department did not believe I would get a well protected patent.
- Its medical department did not think that studies would prove the efficacy of this design.

All three problems and objections were eventually proven to be patently incorrect. Major corporations are inherently adverse to bringing in outside products. The saying goes, "NIH," not in house.

Positive press, television appearances, newspaper interviews, and numerous articles were enjoyed but did not attract a buyer, or more technically a licensee.

In the early 1980s I received a call from Dr. O. Hilt Tatum, a prominent implant dentist from Florida. He had thought of the concept, searched it and found that I owned the Patent rights. He had a small distribution company for a proprietary fluoride and felt this toothbrush would be an easy sell to go with the fluoride.

Concurrently by the 1980s Johnson & Johnson was manufacturing and selling their multi-level toothbrush known as the "Reach." Note: there were no angles. The computerized machinery to make this brush had been built in Brussels, Belgium.

The TB 1 machinery by Boucherie Manufacturing was making the Reach toothbrush in Connecticut, by Johnson & Johnson. Dr. Tatum and I reached an agreement favoring Dr. Tatum's startup and therefore back loaded to me with royalties based on sales over an agreed amount. Dr. Tatum then made his first mistake. He decided to buy his own TB 1 machine and manufacture the toothbrush himself. He could have rented time or paid by the piece on Johnson & Johnson's machinery in Connecticut. He would have freed up money for marketing and advertising, hence his second mistake. He and his sales arm could not get sales up over the minimum in order to trigger royalties. I did get to have toothbrushes of a unique design to hand out to my patients, but once again there was no home run.

In the Spring of 1990, two days after my Patent expired I became aware of Proctor and Gamble's new but very similar toothbrush that was now being marketed. It was a gut blow for sure. Emotionally I was on solid ground but the toothbrush was now seventeen years later and in the public domain. They did legally cite my Patent, which left me frustrated and angry. This is a tough business.

I had another improvement to the original design, called the Force Flex, which bent inward near the leading row of bristles in order to help reach the back of the molars. An example of that toothbrush is in one form or another in today's market place. Another idea was for a plastic triangular toothpick, it, too, is in the market place. The above two items were drawn, signed and dated, but due to patent and development costs, it was not possible to continue with product development, especially without a manufacturing advantage.

In the early 2000s I came up with a cooling device for post chest and thoracic surgery. I found a potential manufacturer in Raleigh, North Carolina, Tom Barnett. He was a Korean War pilot, who had a successful plastics manufacturing plant. During my tour of his plant he took me to see a piece of large machinery covered totally with paint of all colors. When I asked him about it, he told his story. Tom, tall, rugged and casually dressed, told me that after the Korean War he finished his degree in chemical engineering and was now working for Monsanto

Corporation. Monsanto was working for Mr. Walt Disney, who was building a hotel in Anaheim, California for guests of his amusement park nearby. Most of the furnishings were futuristic and made of plastic polymers. The process was not working well and time was of essence. Barnett was on the team and said he could solve the problem in a timely fashion—and he did. Disney rewarded him with the rights to fabricate the face masks of Mickey Mouse and all the other Disney cartoon characters. That is what I like to call a "win win" if ever there was one. A nice piece of machinery indeed. Barnett followed my specifications, save for one detail. Instead of a mini compressor, as I had designed, he developed a cooling transfer system using ice. In the one half hour it took to test with an electronic thermometer, to my disappointment, it did not cool sufficiently. Having a quiet compressor bedside in a hospital setting is a challenge and Barnett was not up to it. By proxy we abandoned that project.

There was another idea in the works, the Orthopedic Stent Vent. Oftentimes orthopedic surgery requires transdermal pins for bone or ligament stabilization. The area is then encased with a plaster cast, against which the extended pin can then rub. The movement then translates to the bone and painfully so. The Transdermal Pin Stent Vent would allow the pin to move inside a rubber ribbed cylinder that could compress and expand as well. Tom liked the idea, we again became partners and he built the prototypes. It was exceedingly difficult to set up appropriate and clinically significant studies on a large group of patients. For a medical devise company working with orthopedic surgeons, doing the research, studies and distribution would most probably have worked.

The same problems kept coming up:
- Being too far ahead of our time
- Being ahead of manufacture capability
- Outside the corporate hemisphere
- Financial short falls
- Possibly unpatentable, therefore limited protection
- Necessity for worldwide patents, prohibitive costs

In the corporate world you have an envelope of support around you, financial, legal, marketing, just to mention a few of them. As an individual entrepreneurial inventor, there are many pitfalls and it is a maze of legal, product, production, and financial issues to work around for success. You never have a chance to let your guard down, there is always, always the possibility that someone else in "the world" is working on your idea at the same time. It is hard to go slow, it is safer to put your head down and go full speed ahead.

By the mid 1980s I decided to spend my creative talents on woodworking and that is when I began the dining room ensemble.

During the last decade of the last century as I watched company after company place their similar toothbrushes on the shelves, I began to come to terms with an effort that seemed so right, so spot on but yet saw me on the outside. However outside I was, the inner conflict, the time, the energy and the enormous personal expense, it all had to be reconciled.

I was grateful for:

• Supportive friends

• My excellent Patent and legal team

• My family's patience and admiration. For example, we were away with our grandchildren and they were using my toothbrush as their travel brush, OK. What a feeling!

• My Patients loved the brush and loved the idea that their dentist invented it. As my son has said, it became my brand.

• It is the toothbrush I use every day, to this day.

• I know I helped a lot of people avoid the pain and suffering of periodontal disease.

• I contributed, I helped, I left my mark.

I felt pride, satisfaction and self gratitude.

Think about it, of the seventy two people who cited my Patent and the largest corporations in the world, I am the only one who could have written and documented this story. I thank you for reading.

I was exhausted and done with inventing but not quite. It was shortly after I retired from dentistry and we moved to Taos while working on a furniture project. I was installing fine solid brass hinges made by Brusso in New York City. The slotted screws were hard to drive and if you slipped the screw was easily damaged and useless. How to avoid the slip.

In fine homes furniture hinges, door hinges, electrical outlet covers and switch covers all have slotted screws and they should all be screwed until left with a vertical slot. It is just an aesthetic differentiation of top work done typically for the wealthy.

I had my "Ah Ha" moment, I saw the problem and the solution.

I had my "Aha" moment

I began patent and prototypes in 2003. I knew what I was doing, I was going to hit it hard and fast to reach the finish line.
I spoke with the owner of Brusso Hardware who told me he supplied the Brass and Silicon Bronze hinges to the finest builders of the finest homes in Manhattan. He would be happy to use the screws and drivers but he was not in a position to manufacture them.

I made prototype screws and drivers in my shop and made plans to go to Las Vegas for the International Fastener Show. I struck out with the few American hardware companies left in the United States. At least ninety-five percent of the companies were from the Pacific Rim. I needed only one, so later that afternoon I was thrilled to connect with an interested Chinese manufacturer.

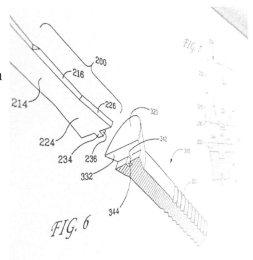

The driver hand or drill bit was easy to make. The screw was not. The screw had the usual slot across and then in the center had a mini rectangular slot that set in below the head and into the shank of the screw. This gave the driver stability and applied to the shank greater driving torque as well. The remaining problem, how to clear the metal out of the indent. Casting was out, as was drilling, which only left stamping.

I received a letter from my Chinese manufacturer. They did not believe stamping would work as there was no where for the excess material to go, as it could not go side to side.

Once again, the devil is in the details. Once again, close but no "cigar."

Better to have tried and failed then not to have tried at all. — SEAN-PAUL THOMAS

Shortly thereafter, a United States Patent was granted for the "Tool Element and Screw of a Mating Engagement Therewith" on April 18, 2006, Patent no. 7,028,592. Inventor, Jeffrey M. Hills.

An idea was developed, drawn, models and prototypes made. The creative process was honored. I am grateful for having had the chance.

In closing, Inventing and being an Inventor is a combination of many fields and attributes:

- Creativity

- Education, formal or otherwise

- Knowledge of the Field of Art

- Problem Solving

- Engineering, at least compatible to what the invention calls for

- Drawing and Model Making

- Emotional Resilience

- Today I would add computer skills extraordinaire

- Essentially an Inventor is a problem solver with creativity and basic skills to put it all together.

To me there is no greater joy than that moment of creativity. To have experienced it fills me with gratitude. I own that personal victory. Once again, I was here, I left my mark.

To me there is no greater joy than that moment of creativity.

Patent Number 3,722,020

United States Patent [19]
Hills

[11] 3,722,020
[45] Mar. 27, 1973

[54] **TOOTHBRUSH WITH CONCAVITY FORMED BY BRISTLE ENDS**

[76] Inventor: **Jeffrey Mark Hills,** 7820 Algon Avenue, Philadelphia, Pa. 19111

[22] Filed: **Jan. 4, 1971**

[21] Appl. No.: **103,591**

[52] U.S. Cl. ....15/167 R
[51] Int. Cl. A46b 9/04
[58] Field of Search ....15/167 R, 167 A, 159 A; 132/84 R; 32/1

[56] **References Cited**

UNITED STATES PATENTS

2,168,964 8/1939 Strasser.................................15/167
3,359,588 12/1967 Kobler..................................15/167 R
1,018,927 2/1912 Savvazin..............................15/167 R
1,753,290 4/1930 Graves..................................15/167 R

Primary Examiner—Leon G. Machlin
Attorney—Lilling & Siegel

[57] **ABSTRACT**

A toothbrush comprising a generally planar head portion having a plurality of bristles forming a concave surface. Some of the bristles are generally perpendicular to said head portion and some are laterally inclined outwardly. This bristle configuration removes food debris, plaque and bacteria lodged in the sulcus area with a minimum of operator manipulation.

10 Claims, 9 Drawing Figures

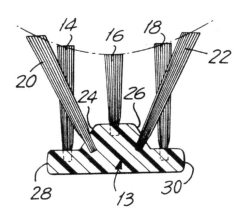

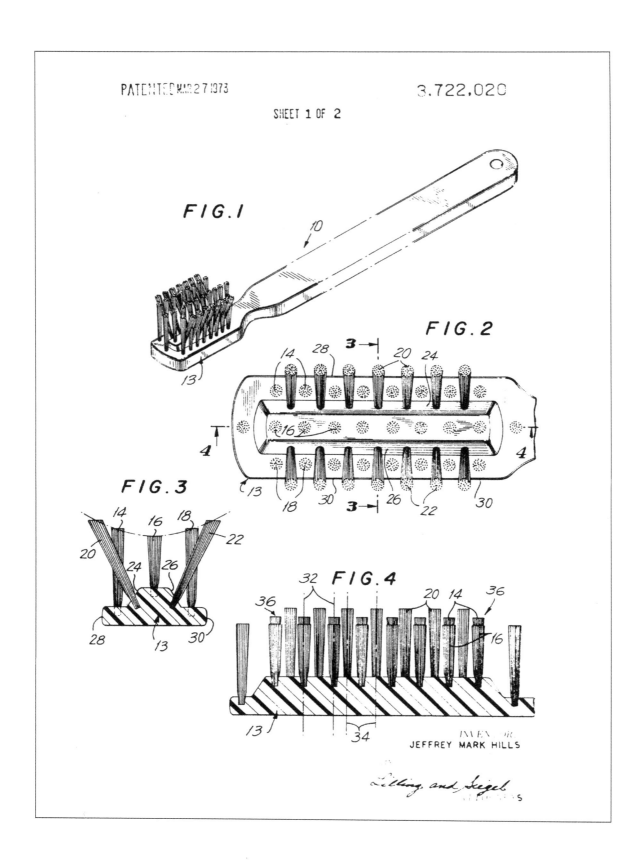

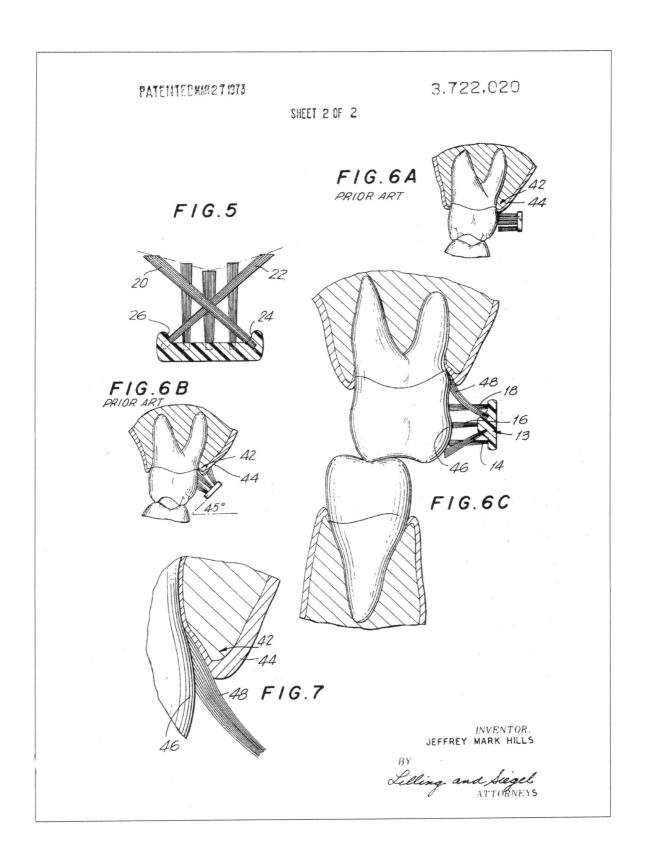

US3722020A - Toothbrush with concavity formed by bristle ends...   https://patents.google.com/patent/US3722020A/en?oq=3722020+

Patents   3722020

Toothbrush with concavity formed by bristle ends

Abstract

A toothbrush comprising a generally planar head portion having a plurality of bristles forming a concave surface. Some of the bristles are generally perpendicular to said head portion and some are laterally inclined outwardly. This bristle configuration removes food debris, plaque and bacteria ledged in the sulcus area with a minimum of operator manipulation.

Images (2)

Classifications

- A46B9/045 Arranged like in or for toothbrushes specially adapted for cleaning a plurality of tooth surfaces simultaneously

View 1 more classifications

Claims (10)

1. A toothbrush, comprising: a head portion having a top surface, a plurality of bristles each extending from on surface to a free end thereof, said bristles being disposed in a number of rows, the locus of substantially all of

US3722020A - Toothbrush with concavity formed by bristle ends... https://patents.google.com/patent/US3722020A/en?oq=3722020+

said rows of bristles extending substantially perpendicularly with respect to said top surface and being dispos
extending at an oblique angle with respect to said perpendicular row, and said two rows of bristles further defi

2. A toothbrush according to claim 1, wherein said substantially perpendicular row of bristles comprise:
and at least one of said oblique rows of bristles comprising means for cleaning sulcus tooth areas.

3. A toothbrush according to claim 1, wherein said head portion is formed with a lower substantially pla
substantially parallel with respect to said lower surface, and first and second inclined surfaces joining s
of bristles extending from said raised surface, a row of said obliquely extending bristles further extendii
toothbrush further including a row of said bristles extending substantially perpendicularly from each of

4. A toothbrush, according to claim 1, wherein the magnitude of said angle is in the range of from 35* tc

5. A toothbrush, according to claim 3, wherein said obliquely extending bristles are longer than said per

6. A toothbrush, according to claim 5, wherein said obliquely extending bristles further extend laterally v
surfaces of said head portion.

7. A toothbrush, according to claim 2, wherein said sulcus cleaning means will engage a user's tooth ar
means is in contact with face surfaces of said same tooth.

8. A toothbrush, according to claim 2, wherein said number of rows is five.

9. A toothbrush, according to claim 8, wherein said rows of bristles comprise two oBlique rows and thre

10. A toothbrush, according to claim 3, wherein each of said oblique rows of bristles extend at an angle
surface.

Description

United-States Patent 91 Hills TOOTHBRUSH WITH CONCAVITY FORMED BY BRISTLE ENDS [76] Inventor: Jeffrey N
[22] Filed: Jan. 4, 1971 [21] Appl. No.: 103,591

[52] US. Cl. ....I5/I67 R [51] Int. Cl. ..A46b 9/04 [58] Field of Search ..15/I67 R, 167 A, 159 A;

[56] References Cited UNITED STATES PATENTS 8/1939 Strasser ..15/167 1 Mar. 27, 1973 3,359,588 12/1967 Kok
1,753,290 4/ 1930 Graves ..15/I67 R Primary Examiner-Leon G. Machlin Att0meyLi1ling & Siegel ABSTRACT A tool
having a plurality of bristles forming a concave surface. Some of the bristles are generally perpendicular to said he
This bristle configuration removes food debris, plaque and bacteria ledged in the sulcus area with a minimum of o

10 Claims, 9 Drawing Figures PATEHTEPHARZYISYS 7 2,020

SHEET 10F 2 /3 INVEN'IOR.

JEFFREY MARK HILLS PATU'HEEWQ? 1373 SHEET 2 BF 2 FIG. 6A

PRIOR/MP7 R. LS

US3722020A - Toothbrush with concavity formed by bristle ends...   https://patents.google.com/patent/US3722020A/en?oq=3722020+

INVE" JEFFREY MARK TOOTHBRUSH WITH CONCAVITY FORMED BY BRISTLE ENDS The invention described here an improved toothbrush head configuration which may be used on hand, electrical or' mechanical toothbrushes.

BACKGROUND OF THE INVENTION The diseases of gingivitis and periodontitis afflict large segments of our popul individual to remove food, bacteria and plaque lodged in the sulcus area between the teeth and the gingivae using pervasiveness of thesediseases must be appreciated.

Uncomplicated chronic marginal gingivitis is the most common disease of the gingivae. It is the initial stage of the irritation, generally in the sulcus area. Gingivitis afflicts 65 percent the the nations school children. Periodontal dis and its prevalence and severity increase with age. The incidence in the 19 to 25 year age group is from to 29 perce disease. The early stage of periodontal disease is gingivitis. At this stage, the gums become tender, swell, bleed a permanently. The teeth then become loose due to loss of supporting bone. There is formation of bacteria-laden p structure for the teeth become so destroyed that extraction and replacement of teeth are required.

The recommended procedure for prevention and treatment of .gingivitis and periodontitis is oral physiotherapy, th toothbrush for cleansing tooth surfaces,'

especially those in contact with the gingivae. Toothbrushing performed shortly after each meal, keeps bacterial ac minimum.

The toothbrushing technique appropriate for use with the conventional toothbrush requires a great deal of operatc the figures of the drawings presented herein will showri and: reference thereof will illustrate the incorrect manner i use with a conventional toothbrush. The error most people make is that the toothbrush bristle ends are placed sut method, the sulcus area between the tooth face and the gingivae is not cleaned when thebrush is moved vertically inclined towards the gingivae by a rotation of approximately 45 from the incorrect substantially square position. W way into the sulcus area. Then, an arcuate motion of the brush head while keeping the bristle ends in place provid supplemented by a motion of the brush in a direction perpendicular to the plane of view (shown in FIGS. 6A and 6I often not possible by. the operator particularly in the molar areas of the mouth and on the inner sides of the teeth.

proper use of this method may do more harm than good. Excessive pressure and/or improper angle of the brush r thereby traumatize them.

There thus remains a need for a toothbrush which will effectively remove food, bacteria and plaque lodged in the s and the primary object of the present invention is to satisfy this need.

More specifically, but still in a broad sense, it is an object of the invention to effectively clean the sulcus area wher most people brush. That is, the cleaning action of the sulcus area should be effective when the brush is held subs either vertical or crosswise.

It is a further object of the present invention that the cleaning action of the sulcus area be effective over a wide ral

It is an additional object of the present invention that in accomplishing the prior stated objects, the risk oftraumati

SUMMARY OF THE INVENTION These objects as well as other objects and advantages which will become appare instant invention which comprises a toothbrush having a generally planar head portion affixed to which are a plura generally perpendicular upstanding from said head portion and are to be positioned substantially squarely against project laterally preferably beyond the sides of said head portion. The inclined bristles are longer than the generall

US3722020A - Toothbrush with concavity formed by bristle ends...   https://patents.google.com/patent/US3722020A/en?oq=3722020+

into the sulcus area automatically at the proper angle and with the proper flexure necessary to achieve a cleansing sulcus area is then effectively cleaned by motion of the brush in any fashion.

The invention will be better understood, and the advantages and objects other than those set forth above will beco description. Such description makes reference to the annexed drawings presenting preferred and illustrative embc

BRIEF DESCRIPTION OF THE DRAWINGS FIG. 1 is a perspective viewof the toothbrush, the

head portion thereof being shown with the bristles pointing upwardly;

FIG. 2 is a plan view of the head portion of the FIG. 7 is a fragmentary view, greatly enlarged of the sulcus area shc

DESCRIPTION OF THE PREFERRED EMBODIMENT Referring to FIG. 1, there is shown a toothbrush 10 having a har portion 13 having a plurality of surfaces, and being of generally planar shape containing preferably three rows of tu perpendicular upstanding. There is also shown a row of tufts of bristles 20 and 22 inclined upwardly and laterally (showing the brush in cross-section makes the new features of the brush of the invention more apparent. Bristle ro rows 14 and 18, respectively. The combination of the three rows of bristles 14, 16, 18 which are substantially perp 12 provide a surface which seats against and is generally conforming to a tooth face. Since the inclined bristles pr the central row of bristles and extend upwards and laterally, preferably beyond the sides of head side surface porti experience a' large component of force perpen-- dicular to them. For this reason only the bristles which are substa position of the brush against the tooth face. The width of the toothbrush head portion is approximately 10 millime millimeters high. The height of the bristle ends above the toothbrush head preferably lies on a laterally concave cu bristle rows 14 and 18 are approximately 1 millimeterhigher than the central bristle row 16. The vertical projection additional 1 millimeter higher. These inclined bristle rows 20 and 22 should preferably extend beyond the sides 28 Such a construction is uniquely novel in that a toothbrush so constructed performs superbly in achieving the objec

It has been found that the angle of elevation of the bristle rows 20 and 22 which are laterally inclined outwardly as the range of from about 50 to about 60. However, angles in the range of from about 35 to about 75 will present the angle and flexure to both achieve a cleaning action and avoid traumatizing the gingivae.

Referring now to FIGS. 2 and 4, the bristles which are substantially perpendicular upstanding preferably lie in an im bristles lie in another imaginary plane numbered 34 in FIG. 41 These two types of planes or rows of bristles prefer toothbrush head. The first and last longitudinal rows 36 should preferably be of those bristles which are substanti portion in order to give additional stability to the seating of the brush against the teeth. The additional bristle tufts portion also lend additional stability.

In FIG. 5, the cross-sectional view of an alternate embodiment, shows the inclined bristles 20 and 22 originating oi and crossing over to the opposite sides. The height of the various longitudinal rows lies on a similar laterally conc FIGS. 3 and 5. In the FIG. 5 modification, the inclined bristles 20 and 22 are longer than in the embodiment of FIG. determination of the seating position of the brush against the tooth face.

The remaining FIGS. 6(A, B and C) and 7 as generally mentioned hereinbefore compare the incorrect and correct u brush of the invention. Thus, FIG. 6A shows that most people incorrectly brush their teeth by holding the bristles 4 therefore, fail to clean the sulcus area 10 by a motion either perpendicular to the plane of view 'or vertical. The app (approximately at 45 with a horizontal) of the brush and an arcuate motion. Here, some bristles find their way into gingivae 44 and thus traumatize them. Furthermore, as previously stated,

US3722020A - Toothbrush with concavity formed by bristle ends...   https://patents.google.com/patent/US3722020A/en?oq=3722020+

this angulatiori and arcuate motion is not always possible. In comparing FIGS. 6C and 7, it will be noted that in the
16, 18 are generally vertically upstanding from the generally planar head portion 13 and preferably form a laterally
against the tooth face 46 while the inclined bristle row 48 readily cleans the sulcus area of plaque, bacteria and fo
arcuate. The angle and flexure of the inclined bristle row which tends to enter the sulcus area is automatically dete
substantially perpendicular upstanding. Thus, the risk of piercing the gingivae 44 is greatly minimized.

After reading the foregoing detailed description, it should be apparent that the objects set forth at the outset of the
while the invention has been shown, illustrated, described and disclosed in terms of embodiments or modification
invention should not be deemed to be limited by the precise embodiments or rriodifications herein shown, illustrat
or modifications intended to be reserved especially as they fall within the scope of the claims here appended.

What is claimed is:

I. A toothbrush, comprising: a head portion having a top surface, a plurality of bristles each extending from one en
said surface to a free end thereof, said bristles being disposed in a number of rows, the locus of substantially all o
least one of said rows of bristles extending substantially perpendicularly with respect to said top surface and bein
bristles each extending at an oblique angle with respect to said perpendicular row, and said two rows of bristles fu

2. A toothbrush according to claim 1, wherein said substantially perpendicular row of bristles comprises means fo
and at least one of said oblique rows of bristles comprising means for cleaning sulcus tooth areas.

3. A toothbrush according to claim 1, wherein said head portion is formed with a lower substantially planar surfac
substantially parallel with respect to said lower surface, and first and second inclined surfaces joining said lower a
of bristles extending from said raised surface, a row of said obliquely extending bristles further extending from ea
toothbrush further including a row of said bristles extending substantially perpendicularly from each of said lower

4. A toothbrush, according to claim '1, wherein the magnitude of said angle is in the range of from 35 to 75.

number of rows is five.

9. A toothbrush, according to claim 8, wherein said rows of bristles comprise two oblique rows and three perpendi

10. A toothbrush, according to claim 3, wherein each of said oblique rows of bristles extend at an angle from and \
surface.

Patent Citations (4)

Publication number	Priority date	Publication date	Assi
US1018927A *	1911-07-14	1912-02-27	Jule:
US1753290A *	1928-11-30	1930-04-08	Lynu
US2168964A *	1937-08-12	1939-08-08	Firm

US3722020A - Toothbrush with concavity formed by bristle ends...   https://patents.google.com/patent/US3722020A/en?oq=3722020+

Publication number	Priority date	Publication date	Assi
US3359588A *	1964-12-14	1967-12-26	Kobl

Family To Family Citations

* Cited by examiner, † Cited by third party

Cited By (72)

Publication number	Priority date	Publication date	Assignee
US3792504A *	1972-09-25	1974-02-19	D Smith
US4010509A *	1975-11-25	1977-03-08	Huish Frederic G
DE2652744A1 *	1975-11-21	1977-06-02	Unilever Nv
US4472853A *	1982-04-21	1984-09-25	Samuel Rauch
EP0120831A2 *	1983-02-21	1984-10-03	d'Argembeau, Etienne Yves G. J.
US4706322A *	1985-09-23	1987-11-17	Nicolas Yvon M
US4776054A *	1987-03-04	1988-10-11	Samuel Rauch
US4852202A *	1988-07-21	1989-08-01	Ledwitz Kenenth W
US5046213A *	1990-03-29	1991-09-10	Colgate-Palmolive Company
EP0449655A1 *	1990-03-29	1991-10-02	Colgate-Palmolive Company
US5335389A *	1990-03-29	1994-08-09	Colgate-Palmolive Company
US5392483A *	1994-07-07	1995-02-28	Chesebrough-Pond's Usa Co., Division Of Conopco, Inc.
USD370564S	1995-03-22	1996-06-11	Colgate-Palmolive Company
EP0716821A1	1994-12-16	1996-06-19	CORONET-WERKE GmbH
US5628082A *	1995-03-22	1997-05-13	Colgate-Palmolive Company
USD380903S *	1995-04-19	1997-07-15	Colgate-Palmolive Company

US3722020A - Toothbrush with concavity formed by bristle ends...   https://patents.google.com/patent/US3722020A/en?oq=3722020+

Publication number	Priority date	Publication date	Assignee
USD386314S *	1996-09-05	1997-11-18	Colgate-Palmolive Company
USD386313S *	1996-09-05	1997-11-18	Colgate-Palmolive Company
US5742972A *	1993-11-02	1998-04-28	Gillette Canada Inc.
US5758383A *	1995-12-29	1998-06-02	Colgate-Palmolive Company
US6006394A *	1992-11-02	1999-12-28	Gillette Canada Inc.
US6086373A *	1996-07-25	2000-07-11	Schiff; Thomas
US6115871A *	1998-05-04	2000-09-12	Royer; George R.
USD434563S *	2000-03-07	2000-12-05	Gillette Canada Company
USD434565S *	2000-04-10	2000-12-05	Bojar James A
US6219874B1	1994-07-13	2001-04-24	The Procter & Gamble Co.
US6260227B1	1998-12-31	2001-07-17	Jacqueline Fulop
US6308367B1	1997-11-12	2001-10-30	Gillette Canada Company
US6314605B1	1996-08-02	2001-11-13	The Procter & Gamble Company
WO2002028221A1 *	2000-10-05	2002-04-11	Gillette Canada Company
US6408476B1	1996-01-18	2002-06-25	The Procter & Gamble Company
US20020152570A1 *	1995-12-29	2002-10-24	Douglas Hohlbein
US6514445B1	1996-12-24	2003-02-04	The Procter & Gamble Company
US6564416B1	2000-05-22	2003-05-20	Gillette Canada Company
WO2004037038A1 *	2002-10-24	2004-05-06	Guang Rong Liu
US6928685B1	2001-11-06	2005-08-16	The Procter & Gamble Company
US20050189000A1 *	2001-01-12	2005-09-01	Cacka Joe W.

US3722020A - Toothbrush with concavity formed by bristle ends...   https://patents.google.com/patent/US3722020A/en?oq=3722020+

Publication number	Priority date	Publication date	Assignee
US20050210612A1 *	2001-07-03	2005-09-29	Colgate-Palmolive Company
US20060242778A1 *	1999-06-14	2006-11-02	Solanki Sanjay A
WO2007033745A1	2005-09-22	2007-03-29	Braun Gmbh
WO2007071031A1 *	2005-12-22	2007-06-28	2062745 Ontario Incorporated
US20090025162A1 *	2003-04-23	2009-01-29	John Geoffrey Chan
US7721376B2	2002-09-20	2010-05-25	Colgate-Palmolive Company
US20120324668A1 *	2011-06-21	2012-12-27	Stofko Joseph A
US8393042B2	2002-08-09	2013-03-12	Colgate-Palmolive Company
US8561247B2	2002-08-09	2013-10-22	Colgate-Palmolive Company
US8800093B2	2002-08-09	2014-08-12	Colgate-Palmolive Company
US8806695B2	2002-08-09	2014-08-19	Colgate-Palmolive Company
US8876221B2	2002-08-09	2014-11-04	Colgate-Palmolive Company
US8943634B2	2011-05-02	2015-02-03	Water Pik, Inc.
US8990996B2	2002-08-09	2015-03-31	Colgate-Palmolive Company
US20160100679A1 *	2014-10-09	2016-04-14	David Hyun Jong Cho
US9468511B2	2013-03-15	2016-10-18	Water Pik, Inc.
USD785947S1 *	2011-03-31	2017-05-09	Obschestvo S Ogranichennoj Otvetstvennostju "Evrocosmed-Stupino"
US9987109B2	2013-03-15	2018-06-05	Water Pik, Inc.
USD844997S1	2016-12-15	2019-04-09	Water Pik, Inc.
USD845636S1	2016-12-15	2019-04-16	Water Pik, Inc.
US10449023B2	2015-07-08	2019-10-22	Water Pik, Inc.

US3722020A - Toothbrush with concavity formed by bristle ends...   https://patents.google.com/patent/US3722020A/en?oq=3722020+

Publication number	Priority date	Publication date	Assignee
US10561480B2	2016-05-09	2020-02-18	Water Pik, Inc.
US10610008B2	2016-12-15	2020-04-07	Water Pik, Inc.
USD897685S1 *	2018-11-16	2020-10-06	World Wide Daily Holdings Company Limited
USD897684S1 *	2018-10-09	2020-10-06	World Wide Daily Holdings Company Limited
USD897686S1 *	2018-12-14	2020-10-06	World Wide Daily Holdings Company Limited
USD897687S1	2018-12-14	2020-10-06	World Wide Daily Holdings Company Limited
USD898372S1 *	2019-01-10	2020-10-13	World Wide Daily Holdings Company Limited
USD898371S1 *	2018-11-16	2020-10-13	World Wide Daily Holdings Company Limited
USD898369S1 *	2018-10-09	2020-10-13	World Wide Daily Holdings Company Limited
USD898370S1 *	2018-10-09	2020-10-13	World Wide Daily Holdings Company Limited
USD906687S1	2019-01-10	2021-01-05	World Wide Daily Holdings Company Limited
EP3838066A1 *	2010-06-25	2021-06-23	Swimc Llc
USD927191S1 *	2018-12-14	2021-08-10	World Wide Daily Holdings Company Limited
US11684142B2 *	2020-02-20	2023-06-27	Anne Ezell

Family To Family Citations

* Cited by examiner, † Cited by third party, ‡ Family to family citation

Similar Documents

Publication	Publication Date	Title
US3722020A	1973-03-27	Toothbrush with concavity formed by
US2161349A	1939-06-06	Tooth brush
RU2021744C1	1994-10-30	Toothbrush head (variants)

Part III

Find your talent, treat it with integrity and hard work and you will have found the meaning to Kahlil Gibran's adage, *work is love made visible.*

— JMH

1951 1970s 1980s 2000s

LAS MANOS DEL HOMBRE
Woodworking

My earliest memories, living in an apartment building, 322 Rockaway Parkway in Brooklyn: I recall being young, four- or five-years old perhaps—there was a hammer in my small hand and a piece of wood on the floor of the hall just outside our apartment. In a primal way I raised that hammer with a dark wooden handle and stroked it down, to see and hear the "thawank" of metal hitting a piece of wood trapped by the concrete below, awesome to my young self.

I certainly wasn't building anything but my hand held and used a tool. Of course, today I can look back and imagine a caveman holding a club, of stone or of wood, and pounding. Was it a small animal needed for sustenance? Was it to grind a grain, a nut to open something like a coconut? For what purpose I know not, but I do know of the sensation of hand on club stroking down, that I know.

My hand holding a tool, over a life spanning eight decades. From woodworker to dentist and back to woodworker again, always a visceral and visual intimacy of a hand grasping a tool. Ironically and no coincidence my two mechanical Patents were both of tools that could be grasped and used to a mechanical advantage.

At around age nine or ten my family moved to Long Island, just as my Brooklyn Dodgers moved to Los Angeles. I was leaving my beloved Brooklyn, as my beloved Dodgers were leaving as well. Pure heartache.

Still not a teen, I began to take books out of the library. My favorites—cars, baseball and woodworking tools. My father needed small lockable boxes for his business; here is where I step in with purpose. Back in the 1950s fruit and vegetable produce was delivered to markets in wooden crates that were discarded when empty. Raw materials were never so inexpensive. To facilitate this production, enter my first power tool, a Shopmate jig saw. My fascination with hand tools was still begging for attention. As it happens my paternal grandfather was a mechanic for a toy company in Brooklyn. He bought most of his supplies from a hardware store in Brooklyn, which was still in business. So here is this eleven-year old alongside his father buying his first tool, a brace, a hand tool that can be used to drill real big holes. The Amish use it in their peg construction post and beam barns. The pegs are then hammered in using large wooden mallets to drive the tapered pegs to join large beams to posts. I have had this brace for over seventy years; I cannot recall using it once. However, to this day I think it looks great and can do a cool thing in a really cool way. Maybe I will put a bit in it and build a project around it someday.

The books I was reading described all sorts of hand tools and I became obsessed with owning them all. Once when wanting some obscure tool my Mother asked a much older cousin of hers, "Why does he need that?" I still remember his supportive answer, "I don't know for sure, but who knows where it will go."

I got the tool while my friends got their favorite toys and games. I began installing molding and trim work for neighbors and friends. Repairing bikes and flat tires for the neighborhood kids. As long as I had a tool in my hands all things were possible.

As long as I had a tool in my hands all things were possible.

My neighborhood friends and I started playing bicycle polo with a ball and crude sticks to whack away. This soon evolved to roller skates and an elementary attempt at street hockey. There were two parallel curbs and two diagonal driveway entrances for goals. What we did not have were pucks and sticks. Well you will recall the produce crates, you can cut them up and you can fashion pucks and sticks. The sticks were big and clumsy and did not last long, but they worked and the price was right. We had a blast, including scrapes and bruises.

When my street hockey buddy Peter and I were in high school we played semiprofessional roller hockey at the local roller rink, coached and played by Dave Warner of Olympic roller dancing pairs with his wife. We traveled to other rinks in New York and New Jersey to play other teams. I wasn't great but the experience stayed with me.

Later in college a bunch of guys formed the Hofstra Ice Hockey club. I played with the same childhood friend, Peter, from the streets of East Meadow, Long Island.

Back to high school and shop class, which we were required to take even as scholastic students. "Shop" was by definition, a semester of wood shop and a semester of metal shop. They both required hand and eye work but the sawdust covered hardwood floors of the wood shop seemed to resonate with me. My main wood project was a memo roll note pad, made of Maple with a Shellac finish and sweet flawless workmanship. In metal shop I made a miniature wheelbarrow, with rivets and spot welds, sprayed black with gold highlights. The piece was perfect and I still have it. How it was not lost is beyond me, but I am grateful to have it.

As I said in an earlier chapter, it was shock and surprise at my high school awards assembly when I was awarded The New York State Steering Commission Award for best high school student in Industrial Arts.

I was awarded The New York State Steering Commission Award for best high school student in Industrial Arts.

In the spring of my senior year of college I proposed marriage to my girlfriend, Phyllis. That summer, without two nickels to rub together, we made our first apartment's furniture in the evenings after work, Phyllis helped with glue ups and sanding. Pine was all we could afford, so pine it was. I recall the neat and tight knots and fine grain. Pine has a nice pitchy smell, much like pinion. When selecting pine you are also selecting an early American or colonial style, which will be distressed, stained a light to medium brown. This stain coincidentally goes by the name "Early American." We designed and built some night tables to go with the headboard we made, as well as a hope chest, coffee table, and a round dining table. Everything was simple and functional. Interestingly, nothing remains today, which is understandable as my woodworking was rudimentary at best.

By 1975 we had moved to our first home, with our firstborn son, Brett, full of adventure and curiosity. It was a basic tract home. Four bedrooms, three baths, kitchen, den with fireplace, living room. and dining room. Shortly after our move we had our second child, Rachael, a bubbly and energetic daughter. We soon decided to open my dental practice in nearby Spring House, Pennsylvania, a sleepy suburb of Philadelphia. With our family of four and a dog we decided to explore the area for land to build our home to raise our children in.

By this time I had subscribed to my first issue of *Fine Woodworking* magazine (of which I have fifty years worth of issues). I read all of master woodworker James Krenov's A Cabinet*maker*'s Note*book:* three volumes full of the art, techniques, and philosophy of a furniture maker. I had caught the bug. I wanted to build furniture and do it well, very well. In 1976 I designed and took on a challenging project. An Oak music cabinet with a roll top. I had a small shop in an alcove in back of our unheated garage with but one stationary power tool, a table saw. I drew extensive plans and incorporated some advanced joinery. The doors were mitered with artisan designed and fabricated stain glass panels.

These stain glass door panels are extensively described in the chapter, "A Special Museum Leads to a Special Visit."

Although it was my very first piece, it had a presence and character, so much so that we decided to submit it to Design Book II, to be juried and, we hoped, accepted and chosen for publication in *Fine Woodworking Magazine's Design Book II, The Best of Furniture* in 1976. It was accepted. We still have this piece today. It holds our picture albums (precomputer) and our memories, certainly a special purpose for a special oaken piece.

Dining Table: the next piece in my garage work shop. A dining table seating for ten, in rosewood, walnut, and glass. Not too far from home there was a store front lumber purveyor on Main Street in Hatfield, Pennsylvania.

I passed by one day and saw some beautiful reddish lumber in the window display, as though they were selling shoes. After I found some metered parking I entered the "store"—mind you this was not a lumber yard, just a small retail store selling exotic imported hardwoods. Just what I needed! By some stroke of good luck they had Brazilian rosewood. Not just a piece or two but the better part of a tree. It was richly figured with matching pieces. It was way more than I needed but I would take care of that later. How I ever brought it home I can not recall, nor can I recall how I ever paid for it. Maybe both for the better.

The table has three unique design elements. Although they work independently, they become a delightful and harmonious design in the completed piece.

The base is a representational tree on each side, with an interior routing for hundreds of Rosewood slats, each hand planed to a bevel on all four edges. The slats were fed into the mirrored and parallel grooved routings. They can readily be seen from the outside. Design element two is where the magic happens. The top of the table is comprised of four slabs of Rosewood (imagine a picture frame) with a rectangular piece of plate glass set in. If an ordinary light or lamp was above the table the light would reflect off the glass, much like a mirror. In the 1970s Lightolier, a lighting fixture company, made a track fixture, dubbed a Pan Parabolic. Essentially an ordinary tungsten bulb goes in a highly polished arm swung under the bulb which reflects light upwards to another polished concave oval, which in turn reflects diffuse light rays downward. Enabled by their diffused beam, the light can penetrate the rectangular glass on top and brilliantly highlight the rosewood slats curving sinuously to the organic shape of the tree. The hundreds of hand-planed edges break the visual into a harmonic meaningful wholeness much as the branches of a tree relate to one another.

Design element three, the table top. The rosewood, as wide as a large dinner plate cut to a rectangle with four mitered joints and edged on the interior and exterior perimeter with walnut. The walnut is planed downward toward the rosewood top, thereby creating a concave shape that seemingly nestles a dinner plate. After fifty years the beauty and design still is timeless.

The chairs were beyond my skill set at the time. I had read an article on a nearby woodworker with an international reputation. We visited his shop and ordered four walnut Conoid, George Nakashima chairs. Some thirty years later the chairs sold handsomely at auction and my skill set had grown to allow me to replace the four Pennsylvania black walnut chairs with eight Oregon musical grade Claro walnut chairs of the exact same design.

There are three other pieces that I built in the dining room. A James Krenov-inspired stemware cabinet with hand carved handles and shelf supports. The door stops and handles were hand carved as well. Forty-five years later the doors still work to perfection. The cabinet is in rosewood and walnut with glass doors. Then I built a silverware cabinet in birdseye maple, with a rosewood case and walnut base. The drawers are fabricated with hand-cut dovetails and natural wood slides.

The last piece is a hanging wall cabinet in rosewood, walnut and book matched tiger maple doors with hand carved maple pulls.

The surprise design element evolved from a family trip to Lake Powell. The route home takes us east of Moab along the course of the Colorado River. I had heard of a small quaint town just off the beaten path called Castle Rock, Utah. Named after a tall slim spire with a flat top of the same name. I brought home a photo and designed a proportional center door. The door front would be glass etched in the shape and spirit of Castle Rock. This is where the magic starts. The inside base is a step up to the back, the base is covered in dark brown velvet. The back wall is completely covered in a smoke gray mirror. Built in above is a soft 15-watt light, which illuminates the interior ever so softly. On each of the levels of the stepped up base a Nambe candlestick holder sits, to reflect in the mirror, creating an organically representational setting, much like the hoodoos in Bryce Canyon National Park.

The above three pieces have horizontal elements with angled relief planed surfaces. During a houseboat visit to Lake Powell I observed in the heat and quiet of the day, that mesas and buttes were not boxes or cubes. They had a flat top, a vertical drop down to an angled relief, another drop and so forth. I called this my "Mesa Design."

All three of the above pieces are still with this dining room ensemble today and they have been published in *Fine Woodworking* magazine as well as *Woodwork* magazine.

Many of our artistic friends and patrons have said of the dining room, "It is like sitting in a museum." Our current house was built around and designed for this very beautiful furniture ensemble.

On a personal note, it took approximately one year in the shop to build each piece, a labor of time and love. Every gathering of family or friends is special. I know if the furniture could talk I would hear, "Thanks for the second chance (tree to lumber to legacy furniture) and thank you for the laughter and fellowship shared in my presence."

In addition to our dining room ensemble, our bedroom furniture, family room, office, and guest room have all been handcrafted by me, my legacy, my hands, the mark I left says much as the caveman said to us from the cave walls "I was here, I lived and worked, this is my art and talent, let my story be told." (adopted from *The Ascent of Man,* by Jacob Bronowski).

In 2003 we moved to Taos, New Mexico. A hand full of pieces were built to round out our needs. Mostly practical and functional in nature, but serving a purpose has intrinsic value as well.

As the 2000s wore on I began to get inquiries from folks here in Taos. I also took my photos and visited galleries. I was represented in three galleries in the course of two or three years with no success. Some of my designs were heavy but not nearly as the locally popular Spanish style furniture. I began work on creating a lighter feel to the table legs and tops. Since the 1980s I had incorporated leg tapers and arches. It was not too much of an effort to design cross members to support a top. This was the beginning of a beautiful gallery piece, the Hall Table, which featured stunning table tops in a variety of species.

While my Taos gallery experience was not doing well I was approached by a local crisis counselor. He knew of my craftsmanship through my homebuilder. A young Pueblo Native American teenage girl was randomly and tragically shot while at a party. Her family was planning her funeral, to be held at the Taos Pueblo Church with her internment to follow in their sacred burial grounds. They requested a hand carved cross with her name carved in the mahogany wood. I designed the piece, after approval I set to work. I was asked to bring it to the entrance of the church courtyard on Saturday at 9:30 am.

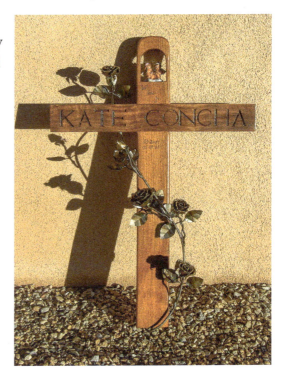

The counselor met me there with the family, and they requested that I carry the cross through the inner courtyard into the Church, down the center isle and sit with it on the stage during the service. I was both honored and ever so slightly uncomfortable given the tragedy leading to this somber service. Here is a Jewish man, who is a carpenter, born in Brooklyn, building and carrying a large cross on his shoulder while participating in a Pueblo Native American burial service. After the service we then marched from the church to the cemetery and past the ancient original burned out church from a war two centuries prior. Now I was in the cemetery and was told that it was hallowed ground, for Pueblo's only, no Anglos. The exception of my being there was not lost on me. I was moved, a tear left my eye. I helped to affix the cross to the post end in the ground, the drilling, driving the screws in, the sun on my back, the stillness only broken by the grief and sobs of the family and friends, the mountains rising high above.

This was a moment of pain, art, and culture intersecting to be remembered to be told as Native Americans, Pueblos and an Anglo man, as a story to be passed on to the next generation. The man from Brooklyn, New York, did not ask for any money, did not receive any money. I was part of something meaningful and spiritual, payment in full.

As time went by I went with Phyllis to visit galleries. I would meet the artists. After pleasantries and small talk I would broach the subject of barter—furniture for art (this being a well know Taos tradition). It worked very well and I was given the opportunity to hone my skills, building furniture for Taos artists as well as to fill our walls with beautiful Taos art. My confidence grew as well as my skill set.

Taos Invites Taos was held every year at holiday time. I soon became aware that the jurors of the show presented awards in a variety of categories. With my best efforts I did my best work, building a pair

> My confidence grew as well as my skill set.

of night stands with each having one drawer. The top was affixed with dovetails, hand cut and fitted. The same construction for the drawer. A master piece in design and craftsmanship. I was so proud to be awarded the distinction of "Taos Living Master" by the Taos Fall Arts Foundation. To this day, so appreciative and honored.

Phyllis and I decided to go to Santa Fe one gray and cold December day. We walked the streets and visited the galleries. As the gray afternoon wore on Phyllis' woolen sweater became wrinkled and bothersome. We were passing the Wiford Gallery on Canyon Road and stopped in for Phyllis to enjoy a bathroom break and fix her sweater. It was a very nice and pricey gallery. While admiring the art I was approached by a tall, handsome sales person, or so I thought. After some small talk I moved on to tell him of my work. He sat down at his desk and he began to listen intently. I had but minutes to cover history, wood species, joinery, and design philosophy. A customer could walk in at any moment. I noticed as I spoke that he began to type on his computer and stare at the screen. After a few moments he looked up at me, "I have been looking at your website, your work is beautiful, stunning in fact. He went on about the furniture and then, "But what really impresses me is your passion, it is exceptional and speaks volumes about you and your work. I would like to represent you and have your work here in the Gallery." Stunned, mouth agape, here I was with a gallery in Santa Fe on Canyon Road. When I could open my eyes and close my mouth, Phyllis was there, having finished her visit to the bathroom. In the short course of that bathroom visit, I went from an artisan of near obscurity to a named artist on Canyon Road. Google had a new entry.

Although Wiford and I had the best of intentions, my work was not a good fit for that gallery. Sales were few and far between. I did, however, enjoy doing construction projects for Tim and his gallery, but this was neither his nor my goal.

The Gallery manager at the time was Michael Galya, a young man with a charming personality and intense focus. He was both knowledgeable and articulate. A few months later he had decided to open his own gallery in Cherry Creek, Denver, and invited me to join him. Luca Decor was on the map. The location, near my daughter could not be more convenient, given its location 270 miles from home. For a multitude of reasons Cherry Creek did not work out. So, it was back to Canyon Road to follow Michael's dream. Michael rented a small gallery but big enough to host a nice collection, about half way up the arty road.

It took Michael only two years to out grow his first location. Fortuitously a space opened at 225 Canyon Road near Paseo de Peralta and at the head of this prominent "gallery" road. This new space, bright and sunny, was at least four times as large as the last location with great parking. New terrific artists were brought in, woodworkers as well. Michael had me focus on coffee and hall tables, as well as George Nakashima-inspired benches with thick live edges and compound bridal joinery. The most challenging—a bridal joint, which is most prevalent in Japanese ultra fine woodworking. When done properly screws and glue are hardly necessary.

My tables were also taking on a new air of evolved sophistication. Beautiful species and the best examples of these fine exotics. In addition to my use of a darker, usually wenge back edge, there was the smaller and proportional front edge,

143

as well as a reflective arch inlay glued into the top at the same corresponding curvature as the front arch connecting the legs.

With an inner satisfaction, Michael often comments that I have been with him from the "beginning" of his gallery ownership. If I should come into the gallery and Michael is with a client, he will introduce me, "Oh, here is the artist, Jeff Hills." It has been over ten years, and I still pinch myself and flush with pride. From the little lad banging with a hammer, who would believe I could do this.

As I am not on the sales floor I rely on others to connect with the clients, sell, and ship. Consequently my work goes into the gallery and then goes out, without any of my contact or personalization. There are custom commissions and at times client connections, which prove to be very satisfying.

One in particular stands out. A couple with homes in Dallas and San Francisco bought a quilted maple coffee table for their San Francisco music room. They then needed a sculpture stand for a "musical rock," A pattern of light is directed upwards, the intensity and pattern is synchronized to the pitch, volume, harmony, etc., of the music. It is as though the rock was part of the music and that is exactly what it is. An artisan from San Francisco was contracted for the stone work, lighting, and wiring. I was contracted to build a walnut lecture stand which would hold this electrical sculpture perfectly. Although quite the undertaking I received great support from my San Francisco counter part.

After delivery I was so delighted to receive a note from the clients to Michael, which read in part, "Jeff is a genius in wood." Most satisfying and I am confident that the fine people from all corners of our country and Europe who have bought my work from Michael's Luca Decor Gallery have spent their money well and have enjoyed their works of art immensely and for all the years to come.

Every holiday season, after having been juried in, we participate in the "Loving Hands of Taos Artists" Stables Gallery holiday gift show. I will do small, medium and large cutting, serving or charcuterie boards.

I make these from multi-species of wood in vibrant colors. Again, I do not generally make personal contact with the buyers. However, on one occasion I received a call from our show director, who was most excited. "Jeffrey, Julia Roberts was just in the Gallery and she bought one of your large serving boards! I smiled broadly, lifted my chest with pride and said 60s style, "Hey that's so cool." Contacts with Gallery clients are very few and far between, but when they come they are so very special and appreciated.

How can something as common place as a chair be so special? Many years ago I began to market The Taos Woodshop for furniture repair and restoration. It became a booming business, and a surprise mystery to me. Then I realized that most people and their furniture came from more humid states than the desert Southwest. The antiquated horse hide glue as well as the moisture content of the wood, would dry out, leaving a loose joint. Poor construction and poor joinery did not help matters.

Folks would bring their chairs beat up, scratched, shaking in the wind. Unable to sit on or use in any functional fashion and ask me to, "Please fix this for me." I would carefully explain the extensive work and time involved and suggest to them to go to a used furniture shop or a flea market and find a chair for pocket change. The answer invariably came back that the chair was special and a legacy piece. I would then restore the chair and bring it back to life and function. A few anecdotes will help bring all this to light.

A gentleman came to me with an end table all in pieces. "Could I please fix it? The moving company from Rhode Island packed it poorly and it must be restored." "Why is this so important I asked?" He answered, "My great great great grandfather came over on the Mayflower. He was a carpenter and he built this table after he settled in Rhode Island." I restored it both functionally and aesthetically. It was presented to the gentleman with pride. He owns a cafe and ice cream shop in town and should he see me at 9:00 am he will offer me a sweet treat of my favorite flavor ice cream on the house; he is so appreciative.

A woman came to me with a beat up high chair. The paint was dulled by at least one hundred years, legs so loose it could hardly stand. "And why is this so important?" I asked. "My grandfather sat in it as a toddler." I restored the high chair and her heartfelt memory.

One day I got a call from the caretaker at the estate of Millicent Rogers' granddaughter. They had two chairs that needed repair and were her favorites, could I help? We went over in the pickup truck and we were startled by what we saw. Two chairs that were in disrepair, broken down, both physically and aesthetically. These two chairs were original Louis XIV antiques. They were to be brought back to beauty and function!

Another chair repair came from an elderly gentleman who lived in Oklahoma and had a vacation home in Taos. The chair was well made but needed some help, but why? The client drawled, "They were from my father's law firm and he was a United States Senator from Oklahoma. I want to be a good steward of these chairs and his legacy."

The chairs kept coming and so did tables, hope chests, and all manner of furniture, but all the different stories had one common theme. This was legacy furniture, with a story to tell and a history to share. The furniture was passed down and love came with it.

I took pleasure and pride in the process. Mending their legacy furniture and their hearts as well. I felt honored to help in keeping their memories alive.

I was quite good at this furniture repair specialty. I wondered how that happened with no formal education. *Fine Woodworking* magazine would have the occasional article on antique restoration, my dental background helped as well. The most skilled talent was my intuitive nature. If I laid my hand on it, touched it, I could repair it with the stuff in my tool box. Boat building taught me much about working with epoxy. I then took that leap to furniture repair.

I built five boats and all were sea worthy.

I built five boats and all were sea worthy. Here are some of their stories.

In the mid 1980s I decided I wanted to relive part of a trip I did in the 1960s to Expo '67 in Montreal Canada in a 22-foot inboard sterndrive Chris Craft. The most beautiful cruising was on the northern end of Lake Champlain, the

port of entry to Canada, Rouses Point, to the River Richelieu with all its locks. Phyllis and I ordered a kayak kit for two. We built, outfitted, and supplied this small vessel for a one-week round trip south to north on this south to north flowing river. From Rouses Point we traveled north on the river and with difficulty we would get the attention of the lockkeeper to open the gate. As they were done by hand with large wheels, we would be lucky to get a two-foot opening. Knowing where we were on the water and where our hotels were was quite the challenge. Fortunately for the most part the roads were near and parallel to the river, from where we could read the road signage.

After a day of paddling what a relief to find our town and hotel. First problem, in the rain carrying the kayak up a steep and slippery embankment. Second problem, carry the loaded kayak across a four-lane, well-trafficked divided highway. The hotel helped us store the boat and took us to a small family French restaurant, "The Imprevu." I fell in love for the second time in my life, French cuisine.

Next we paddled to the beautiful Bassin de Chambly. The wind was blowing but the current was still with us. We decided to spend the night and asked the local innkeeper for a hotel suggestion up north. He recommended a Relais resort on the water's edge. After a day of paddling we knew when we arrived by the beautiful boats tied up on the docks. We also knew that after three days of paddling in the rain it was time for a vacation. The notion of paddling against the current for the return trip was weighed against the ambience of staying at the Relais, with its swimming pool, and delicious food, no contest.

While we were getting our gear off the kayak onto the deck we realized there was a "fancy" French wedding taking place. We fit right in with our sea boots and rain gear!

While waiting for our dinner table, glasses of complimentary Veuve Clicquot champagne flowed freely I don't remember dinner, except it was lovely and luxurious, the highlight of the trip. We stayed two days in this ambiance before I took a forty-minute cab ride to Rouses Point to pick up our car for the trip home. A much needed and beautiful memory of "surf and turf."

In 1993 we purchased our first major boat, a 32-foot Island Gypsy trawler, previously owned by an airline pilot. The boat was as "salty as it gets," Teak decks, handrails, transom. and swim platform. The boat needed a dingy in order to get to shore for supplies and the occasional dinner. I also enjoy rowing as an exercise. I thought a 6-foot dingy would do and ordered a kit with "100 pieces." I did some improvising and modifications, varnishing and painting. It rowed decently and looked sharp. It lived on a custom cradle on the stern deck. Dropping it in the water and hoisting it up was safe and manageable with stabilizing rigging off the boom and mainstay. The four-to-one mechanical advantage provided by the two wooden block pulleys was all that was needed to complete this task. As the years went by, I realized six feet of dingy was marginally sea worthy for two. We had to add another two feet. Matters of sea worthiness were getting dicey now. I cut the transom off, and I sanded each plank's end in a semi-circle,

149

reducing the thickness by one half. I counter-sanded the new 2-foot section and epoxied it all together. The hull sides and rails were built to fit. The transom was trimmed down and affixed. A new stern seat was installed and fitted. Now to make it seaworthy while connecting the original six feet to the new two feet—a full length keel.

Constructed with a thick piece of mahogany, properly shaped. Silicon bronze screws and epoxy to fasten it all together. Repainted flag blue and with marine varnish for the rest. It looked great. I submitted it to Wooden Boat magazine and they published it in the next issue, in the "Re-Launch" sections with pictures.

Shortly after moving to Taos my yearning to be on the water grew stronger by the day. We decided to build a boat that would be ideal for our local lakes, both for sailing and rowing. Research led me to an Annapolis, Maryland naval architect, who was selling plans for a 16-foot sailboat. I knew I could also fit it with the proper seat and oar locks as I was building the boat. With plans in hand, a list was formed—teak, mahogany, marine plywood. The mast and boom, Douglas fir from Canada and all sorts of marine epoxy. Phyllis and I set out to build the boat which took approximately 250 hours. It was ready for a late summer launch. I had modified the keel with more "beef" and depth. From fore to aft a silicon bronze band ran along the bottom to protect the hull while allowing for scratch free beaching. I also fiber glassed the forward section of the hull, again to have scratch free beaching. We named the boat "Michiah, Yiddish for "a pleasure."

Although the boat did not sail to the windward quarter well, it rowed beautifully. We would often take turns rowing and handling the tiller, then beach the boat and go for a swim. Heron Lake, the boat and our Safari Airstream made a good team. Unfortunately climate change caught up to the Lake and it is often dry or unhealthy to be on, no less due to an overgrowth of algae. The boat was honored by Wooden Boat magazine and published in its "Launchings" section.

We could not travel to Lake Powell with the Airstream and trailer the 16-foot boat. So I decided to build an 8-foot tender. A company in Gig Harbor, off Puget Sound, Washington, agreed to sell me a bare fiberglass hull. I met the moving truck in the Walmart parking lot here in Taos and we slid it onto the bed of my pickup truck. Once home I built a custom cradle for it and then got to work. All hand crafted Spanish cedar trim, seats, bow, aft quarter corners, bottom paint, two-tone hull sides, interior paint, and lots of high gloss marine varnish. A local sign maker made a gold and red trim vynal, "Michiah" and a set of fine spoon oars from Maine competed the effort. The new 8-foot Michiah was technically the tender to the 16-foot Michiah. The nearby Eagles Nest Lake is cold water and snowmelt filled. It is still in good shape

and holds some hope for time on the water in the future. To this day Gig Harbor Boats uses pictures of the 8-foot tender Michiah on its website as an example of its eight-foot Nisqually, all trimmed out, with hand crafted marine hardwoods.

I never had a formal education in wood work outside of high school, but I have an extensive library, featuring the twentieth century masters, terrific books on tools, techniques and construction. In addition I have approximately fifty years of *Fine Woodworking* magazines. There is a great satisfaction in being self-taught and in building one's environment. What has it meant to me?

I personally believe my hand is an extension of my mind and my heart. When working, the hand must hold a tool. The earliest caveman knew this. A stick, a piece of a tree, a stone, big for smashing, small for a club, or smaller still for an arrow. My favored tools are built in small Japanese towns by generational master craftsman. The steel used must be strong, sharpened to cut like a razor and durable to hold that edge. My chisels are hand hammered, made from extremely hard steel, reclaimed from sunken chains and anchors that have laid in the water a century

My hand is an extension of my mind and my heart

or more. This hardened steel is forged, hammered and sharpened to a razor edge. These are my chisels, I like to chop and do well with these, paired with a Japanese hammer. Planes, Japanese block, in particular, shave, while Japanese saws cut. There you have it. The basics of hand tools. Today, I always cut dovetails by hand. It is enjoyable and it is my "mark," period.

There are five basic joints in wood working. The mortise and tenon, dovetail, miter, dado, and dowel. Just five joints but with many variations. There are many choices in the sharpening of the a fore mentioned tools. There are oil stones, diamond plates, sand paper affixed to glass and others. I use Japanese water stones. They are all in custom boxes and each stone has an appropriate slurry stone in order to make a thicker slurry to run the blade through. Each blade runs through a series of four stones and then red rouge is rubbed on a leather strop for the final polishing step. The tool's edge is sharp enough to pare the hair off your skin.

The final technique lesson: How to measure and cut a line.

After selecting the appropriate ruler, T Square, or right angle square we have three choices in how to scribe this line: with a dull pencil, a sharp pencil, or a sharp marking knife. The narrowest most accurate is the marking knife cut. The line is scribed about 1/100th of an inch in thickness. Goal to cut a piece of wood, say fourteen inches in length and to be able to constantly repeat it. We have three choices, cut right over the line, cut to the right of the line, or make our cut to bisect the line in half. Let's say one two hundredth of an inch. Whether by hand or machine the line scribed is always cut bisected or half way through. Consistency of method, tool, hand and eye working to near perfection. The mark of a craftsman, and the reason why it is the most difficult of joints to make, the dovetail is cut by hand. You are living and practicing integrity through your skills and end product.

A legacy piece of furniture. Beauty to the eye, functional to the body or purpose.

From the beginning I sought the answer to the meaning of it all. Interestingly I have come to realize it's a moving target.

Childhood—Hey I built a hockey stick and a puck, I can play hockey.

As a young adult—I can build a dining table and have a place to eat so let's build it.

As a mid-life adult—I had a creative spirit, I love art, I have talent and a desire for it to learn and grow. I want to build masterpieces.

As a senior today—These master works of craftsmanship add another dimension. The craftsman defined and remembered by his legacy works.

In Jacob Bronowski's *The Ascent of Man* he writes of the early cave men,

> There are many gifts that are unique in man; but at the center of them all, the root from which all knowledge grows, lies the ability to draw conclusions from what we see to what we do not see, to move our minds through space and time, and to recognize our selves in the past on the steps to the present. All over these caves the print of the hand says: "This is my mark, this is man."

He goes on further,

> Now the hand no longer imposes itself on the shape of things. Instead, it becomes an instrument of discovery and pleasure together, in which the tool transcends its immediate use and enters into and reveals the qualities and the forms that lie hidden in the material.

My concluding quote from Bronowski

> ...the hand is the cutting edge of the mind... In the end the march of man is the refinement of the hand in action.

The *Ascent of Man* and how it touches my soul.

> ... the most powerful drive in the Ascent of Man is his pleasure in his own skill. He loves to do what he does well and having done it well, he loves to do it better. You see it in his science. You see it in the magnificence with which he carves and builds, the loving care, the gaiety, the effrontery.

In Bronowski's *The Ascent of Man,* these discoveries are made by people who have two qualities: "An immense integrity and at least a little genius."

On my shop wall for thirty year was a "psychodelic" poster, it said, "Work is love made visible." I took it at face value; was there more to it? Love exists in the emotional world, but it is more than that. The cognitive world of communication, integrity, and vulnerability makes that emotional world so much richer, deeper, and trusting.

As a woodworker my accuracy and my integrity lies in reaching a precision akin to perfection. Who wants sloppy joints, a scratched surface, who would spend hard earned dollars for that? So I strive for perfection, the design, wood selection, construction, and finish. Striving is pushing both mentally and physically, you open your eyes, you look, you see, then it all goes through the cognitive filter of integrity and at this stage, "all while no one is looking," it is but you and your integrity. All the while the objective is perfection, which in itself is both an illusion and a perception of what your eyes and mind can see and interpret through that filter of integrity. Although it sounds like a conundrum, it is rather clear, if you have talent and integrity, you will make art.

As Matthew B. Crawford wrote in, *Shop Class as Soulcraft*, an inquiry into the value of work, "People who make their own furniture will tell you that it is hard to justify economically and yet they persist. Shared memories attached to the material, souvenirs of our lives, and producing them is a kind of communion with others and with the future."

It could not be more lyrically expressed than by Neil Diamond in his song, "Morningside," (Abridged)

> He left a table made of nails and pride, and with his hands he carved these words inside, "for my children …"
>
> And the legs were shaped with his hands and the top made of Oaken wood. And the children sat around this great table touched with their laughter, Ah, and that was good.

The subtitle to this history of my life as a woodworker, at the beginning of this chapter, captured a unique moment in my life as a woodworker and dental healer.

It was the early 1970s and I had just completed a dental procedure on an older Hispanic woman, at our clinic in North Philadelphia. As she was about to leave, she took my hand in hers; they were warm and gentle, her face revealed a combination of relief and gratitude. With her hands holding mine, she locked onto my eyes and said in Spanish, *"Las Manos del Hombre,"*—the hands of the man. It is over fifty-five years later and this frail, older Hispanic patient is remembered and revered by me for having so touchingly effected the arc of my life and so generously touched my heart.

"Things men have made with wakened hands, and put soft life into are awake through years with transferred touch, and go on glowing for long years, and for this reason, some old things are lovely, warm still with the life of forgotten men who made them."

— **DH Lawrence**

Part IV

PHOTO ALBUM **FAMILY AND FRIENDS**

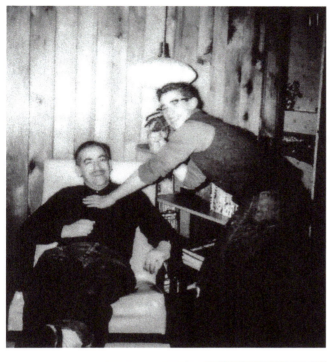

161

"You use a glass mirror to see your face; you use works of art to see your soul."

—George Bernard Shaw

THANK YOU

The first Thank you is a special Thank You and that could only go to my wife, my friend, my muse ... Phyllis. Directly for editing and typing the first four drafts, a true labor and a labor of love.

However, to be perfectly clear, Phyllis was a participant and inspiration in most every story. Either by being in the boat or building the boat. She can drill a hole or drive a screw all while laying under a boat. She can paddle down rapids on the river as well as bike fifty miles.

There is more to my success, it took a special magic. Phyllis can run a house, finances, manage a Dental Practice, do the grunt work and office work needed for my endeavors.

Brett and Rachael needed to get to school and home, to Little League and Gymnastics and the list goes on and on. Through all this mayhem she still found the time to fulfill her dream of completing a Masters in History, an academic milestone at Villanova University. A most heartfelt Thank You to her for help and support of my dreams, which is rightfully our dreams.

To Olivia and Sam for putting the "Gold" in our golden years, you are the best!

To our dear friends Drs. Bennett Gaev, Psychiatrist and his wife Lilly Gaev, Cognitive Behavioral Therapist. Our sincere gratitude for fifty three years of friendship and much like as lives play out, "for better or for worse." We have always been resolved to be for the better. A personal thanks for great books on Psychology, Psychiatry and the human mind to read. Certainly deep and inspiring conversations to share and nourish my curiosity. Happy times to share and help to persevere through the thickets of the difficult times.

Thank you to our longest married friendship and Philadelphia friends, Drs. Murray Cohen and Judy Cohen. Every boat needs an anchor you can trust. Thank you dear friends.

Special Thanks to Dr. Stephen and Barbara Finberg, always there for me always appreciated.

To my "Brother" Peter Dolgoff, after sixty-seven years of friendship we are truly the brothers we never had.

To my partner in friendship and adventure, Mikey Ehrenpreis, sixty-five years and still going.

Thank you to my "health keepers":

Dr. Lucas Schreiber MD, Dr. Lucy Whyte Ferguson DC, Yoga Teacher Raquela Moncada Cowan, Massage Therapist Nadine Lollino, LMT, E-RYT.

Thank you to my writing coach Johanna DeBiase for setting me on my way out of a safe harbor and helping me to hone my writing skills, and to our friend and wellness councilor Michelle Wilde for encouraging me to write this book. To my publisher and cheerleader, Rebecca Lenzini of Nighthawk Press, a bundle of support and knowledge. Our experienced and talented Copy Editor, Anne Flanagan. To our brilliant Jack Leustig of Fine Art New Mexico, who took sixty five years of our pictures both analog and digital, putting them all into the same digital language both improved and formatted for our Art Director, Kelly Pasholk of Wink Visual Arts, to blend our stories and photographs skillfully into the story of our lives.

It has been my pride, my privilege, to my team my gratitude and heartfelt thanks.

Thank you to my children, son Brett and his significant other Maria Chisolm, daughter Rachael and son-in-law Brett Shaheen. Your love, support, and counsel is always valued and appreciated.

To my sister, Michelle Amster, brother-in-law Arnie Amster and to my sweet niece Gina, Rest in Peace. Know that you are remembered.

To my Parents, who held me, encouraged me, nurtured me, loved me... my deepest thanks.

To all my friends and family who have passed to the other side, always in my heart, rest in peace.

In this life I have had the privilege to be addressed as Doctor, Inventor and Artist, and now Author. I am both honored and humbled and please call me Jeff.

ABOUT THE AUTHOR

Jeffrey M. Hills is a first-time book author. Even though he has pursued many adventures as an entrepreneur in his life, he is very excited about this endeavor.

Jeffrey was born in Brooklyn, New York, and his family moved to East Meadow, Long Island, when he was eleven years old. It is said that you can take the "boy" out of Brooklyn but you can not take Brooklyn out of the boy, and so it is.

Jeffrey and his wife Phyllis raised their family, son Brett and daughter Rachael, in Montgomery County outside of Philadelphia. One of many special trips the family took was to Lake Powell living on their house boat.

Jeffrey retired from dentistry in 2003 and he and Phyllis moved to Taos, New Mexico, where they live in the house they designed for the furniture Jeffrey built throughout their life. He loves the West and enjoys tending his orchard of apple, pear, and peach trees. In the winter months he and his wife will cross country ski and bike ski. In the summer they have traveled in their Airstream throughout the West's National Parks and explore on their bicycles. Over the 55 years of marriage Jeffrey and Phyllis have had five dogs and the boy they rescued eleven years ago is a black lab mix named Duke who shares their life and adventures now.

JEFFREY M. HILLS

Born: December 12, 1946, Brooklyn, New York

East Meadow High School, 1964
• New York State Steering Commission Award Excellence
  in Industrial Arts,1964

Hofstra University, BA, 1968
• Who's Who in American Colleges and Universities

Temple University School of Dentistry, 1972
• American Dental Association Scientific Achievement Award
• University of Pennsylvania Advanced Program in Restorative Dentistry
• Boston College, Advanced Program Periodontal Prosthesis
• Fellow of the Academy of General Dentistry, 1984
• American Society for Dental Esthetics Kinetic Cavity Preparation, 1995
• Toothbrush Patent 3,722,020, March 27, 1973
• Screw and Driver Patent 7,028,592 B2, April 18, 2006

Carpentry/Artistry
• Taos Living Master, Fine Furniture, Awarded 2008
• Juried Acceptance to Artful Home, Fine Furniture, 2010
• Represented by Luca Decor Gallery
  Canyon Road, Santa Fe, New Mexico, 2012–Present

Publications
• "Angular Bristle Toothbrush," *Journal of Periodontics*, 1974
• "The Stress Effectors Contributing to Periodontal Disease,"
  Journal of Periodontology
• "Differential Interactive Diagnosis of Carries With Sequentially
  Integrated Treatment"
• *Fine Woodworking Design Book II*, 1979
• Newspaper, magazines, and journals too numerous to mention

Other
• President of the Board, Rocky Mountain Youth Corps, six years
• Treasurer, Childrite Adoption for Special Needs Children
• Landscape Photography, hobbiest/analog camera/fully adjustable
  field camera
• Philadelphia Masters Triathlon, 1982
• Jim Thorpe Anthracite Triathlon—Olympic Level, 1983
• Author, *My Brooklyn Bridge*, 2024

Printed in the USA
CPSIA information can be obtained
at www.ICGtesting.com
LVHW071910030824
787237LV00015B/200